Afoot in England

W. H. Hudson

STANFORDS TRAVEL CLASSICS

BEAUFOY BOOKS

First published in 1909

This edition published in 2010 by
Beaufoy Books
in association with Edward Stanford Ltd.

Copyright © 2010 John Beaufoy Publishing Ltd.
and Edward Stanford Ltd.

Beaufoy Books
11 Blenheim Court, 316 Woodstock Road, Oxford,
Oxon OX2 7NS, UK

ISBN 978-1-906780-24-1

Designed and typeset by Bookcraft Limited, Stroud, Gloucestershire, UK
Printed in India by Replika Press Pvt Ltd.

Contents

Contents

Foreword

What kind of a book is *Afoot in England*? A gazetteer? Certainly not.
A guidebook? No. An antiquarian's dawdle through the English past?
Far from it. A series of amiable ambles, of pilgrimages made in idleness?
Yes, but not only. A manifesto for walking as a way to see the world?
At times. Even Hudson doesn't know how to describe it: the best he
can come up with in the preface is 'an account of the hundred little
adventures met during wanderings...without map or guidebook'. That
modest paraphrase is nearly there, but it still doesn't catch what sets the
book apart from the many other walking-tour travelogues published in
England in the early 1900s.

Three things do so. There is the sharpness of Hudson's eye (brought
up on the pampas of South America, he was an auto-didact natural
historian of serious expertise). There is the sharpness of Hudson's
prose (as novelist, essayist and memoirist he is – along with Richard
Jefferies and Edward Thomas – one of the finest English naturalist-
writers of the late-19th and early-20th centuries). Above all there is
the uncanniness of the English landscape he evokes. For it is a 'deep
England' through which Hudson travels, and from those depths rise
up spectres, ancestors, visitants, memories of violence and episodes
of supernatural beauty. You'll encounter these moments as you read,
but consider yourself warned in advance: what begins, bucolically,
as a leisured countryman's tramp through the southern counties
is quickly ruptured by the mystical-sinister, by visionary raptures
and by eerie time-travels. Hudson knows he is moving over an old
country, whose surface is unstable and prone to collapse. He is
adventuring not in nostalgia, but in something far more volatile
and alarming.

This is the deep-English supernaturalism that repeatedly erupts
into children's literature, in books like John Masefield's *The Box
of Delights*, Joan Aiken's *The Wolves of Willoughby Chase*, Susan
Cooper's *The Dark Is Rising* sequence and even John Wyndham's
The Midwich Cuckoos (in which a sleepy English village becomes
the hatchery for an alien species who lay children with golden eyes
and psychic powers). Like these writers, Hudson is interested in
the unhomeliness that comes when what he calls the 'same familiar

green land' of England, the 'same old country', suddenly develops 'a difference'.

It is in search of these 'differences' that Hudson journeys. Walking is his method or medium: he rambles for weeks, months, seasons, moving 'hither and thither', letting the landscape lead him. He follows the beckonings of the terrain: pursuing ancient drove-roads and holloways, streams and rivers (the River Exe 'leads' him like 'a beautiful silvery serpent'), acting on tip-offs and instinct, waiting for happenstance and alignments to issue into revelation. In this way, he reaches spots in the landscape where, he puts it, you might slip 'back out of this modern world into that of half a thousand years ago'. A kind of pastoral psychogeography, then, with Hudson as the dowser of sites of energy, wandering by chance, waiting for what he calls the 'charm of the unknown' to set his rods quivering (and there we should hear 'charm' not as a synonym for the picturesque, but instead for cantrip, for old magic, for powers of the light and the dark).

So it is, for instance, that when Hudson steps into a village church somewhere in the West Country, in 'On Going Back', the vicar he meets is no beaming dog-collared Anglican, but instead a man whose eyes have a 'strange light in them', whose face is 'cold' and 'ascetic', and who speaks to Hudson of toads and reptiles. Out on the Norfolk coast he finds holiday-makers who appear to him like 'a herd of large beautiful white cows', with 'large light-blue eyes', sinister in their calmness. Elsewhere, he sees silent villagers who resemble 'interred bodies from the Bronze Age' that have 'now come out of their grave and put on modern clothes'. In the book's most disturbing and unrationalised encounter, he follows an old road and along it finds a 'little farm-house'. Thirsty, he knocks on the farm-house door in the hope of begging a glass of milk, and is met by a young woman with 'a colourless face', who speaks 'mechanically' and is incurious as to Hudson's presence, but clearly desirous that he leave as soon as possible. The encounter 'chills' Hudson's blood, and makes 'the heat out-of-doors seem grateful' to him (fortunately, he is soon afterwards restored by an invigorating encounter with two 'comely Devon women').

People in *Afoot in England* often threaten Hudson, but nature always reassures him – and at times transfigures him such that he becomes a 'burning and shining spirit', and his physical matter 'but a disguise, a shadow and delusion'. The book in part records the quest of a naturally solitary man to find solace and company in small-scale wild places. A stretch of heath or a fragment of woodland offers him 'an oasis and a refuge'. Open country brings back to him 'the sense of lost liberty'. 'We feed our sick souls with the ocean', he reflects during an early chapter. This is nature as psychotherapy, and as such a familiar preoccupation of the English travel-writer. Far more radical, however, are the moments at which Hudson describes himself overwhelmed by a neo-Platonic mysticism, whereby the natural world and the human body remain only as shadow-plays for a 'universal soul'.

Nature-mysticism tendrils its way through all of Hudson's imaginative writing, surging out most obviously in his novel *Green Mansions*. Hudson was obsessed with greenness as a cognate both for truth (a version of Hildegaard of Bingen's *viriditas*) and for natural energy. Indeed, I sometimes imagine him – with his luxuriant beard, his powerful chlorophyllia, his *enfant sauvage* childhood on the pampas – as an Edwardian Green Man, striding the land, speaking in leaves, always on the point of transmigration into plant or creature.

The book's most remarkable scene of transmigration occurs on the North Sea coast. Hudson is in East Anglia on a hot day, at a calm low tide, and is watching herring gulls on the long blond sands. Suddenly a 'soft bluish silvery sea-haze' appears, which causes sky, water and land to 'blend and interfuse', producing a 'new country that was neither earth nor sea'. The haze also magnifies the gulls until they seem no longer 'familiar birds', but 'twice as big as gulls, and...of a dazzling whiteness and of no definite shape.' They temporarily appear to Hudson as ghost-gulls or spirit-birds 'that lived in or were passing through the world', presences made briefly visible by the haze. Then, in a brilliant reversal, he imagines that he himself, 'standing far out on the sparkling sands, with the sparkling sea on one side', is also dematerialised:

> If any person had looked at me from a distance he would have seen me as a formless shining white being standing by the sea, and then perhaps as a winged shadow floating in the haze. It was only necessary to put out one's arms to float. This was the effect on my mind: this natural world was changed to a supernatural.

'A winged shadow floating in the haze': Hudson was first and always a bird-man, and dreams of flying haunt his books, as real birds flock in them. In the 1890s, walking the high chalk paths of the South Downs, he experienced an illusion of aeriality so intense that he 'almost realise[d] the sensation that ... I shall lift great heron-like wings and fly with little effort to other points of view'. In *Afoot in England* he calls birds 'feathered people'; they are, to him, companionable. But they are also inspiring, in the promises they issue of elevation and of revelation. One of the many reasons why *Afoot in England* makes such compelling reading is the sense of Hudson's volatility as a presence and a mind. Reading it, you feel that he might at any moment transmigrate, swap his species, and lift off in bird-form, or even evaporate into 'a beautiful mist of atmosphere'.

Robert Macfarlane, May 2010

CHAPTER ONE

Guide-Books: An Introduction

Guide-books are so many that it seems probable we have more than any other country – possibly more than all the rest of the universe together. Every county has a little library of its own – guides to its towns, churches, abbeys, castles, rivers, mountains; finally, to the county as a whole. They are of all prices and all sizes, from the diminutive paper-covered booklet, worth a penny, to the stout cloth-bound octavo volume which costs eight or ten or twelve shillings, or to the gigantic folio county history, the huge repository from which the guide-book maker gets his materials. For these great works are also guide-books, containing everything we want to learn, only made on so huge a scale as to be suited to the coat pockets of Brobdingnagians rather than of little ordinary men. The wonder of it all comes in when we find that these books, however old and comparatively worthless they may be, are practically never wholly out of date. When a new work is brought out (dozens appear annually) and, say, five thousand copies sold, it does not throw as many, or indeed any, copies of the old book out of circulation: it supersedes nothing. If any man can indulge in the luxury of a new up-to-date guide to any place, and gets rid of his old one (a rare thing to do), this will be snapped up by poorer men, who will treasure it and hand it down or on to others. Editions of 1860–50–40, and older, are still prized, not merely as keepsakes but for study or reference. Any one can prove this by going the round of a dozen second-hand booksellers in his own district in London. There will be tons of literary rubbish, and good stuff old and new, but few guide-books – in some cases not one. If you ask your man at a venture for, say, a guide to Hampshire, he will most probably tell you that he has not one in stock; then, in his anxiety to do business, he will, perhaps, fish out a guide to Derbyshire, dated 1854 – a shabby old book – and offer it for four or five shillings, the price of a Crabbe in eight volumes, or of Gibbon's *Decline and Fall* in six volumes, bound in calf. Talk to this man, and to the other eleven, and they will tell you that there is always a sale for guide-books – that the supply does not keep pace with the demand. It may be taken as a fact that most of the books of this kind published during the last half-century – many millions of copies in the aggregate – are still in existence and are valued possessions.

There is nothing to quarrel with in all this. As a people we run about a great deal; and having curious minds we naturally wish to know all there is to be known, or all that is interesting to know, about the places we visit. Then, again, our time as a rule being limited, we want the whole matter – history, antiquities, places of interest in the neighbourhood, etc.- in a nutshell. The brief book serves its purpose well enough; but it is not thrown away like the newspaper and the magazine; however cheap and badly got up it may be, it is taken home to serve another purpose, to be a help to memory, and nobody can have it until its owner removes himself (but not his possessions) from this planet; or until the broker seizes his belongings, and guide-books, together with other books, are disposed of in packages by the auctioneer.

In all this we see that guide-books are very important to us, and that there is little or no fault to be found with them, since even the worst give some guidance and enable us in after times mentally to revisit distant places. It may then be said that there are really no bad guide-books, and that those that are good in the highest sense are beyond praise. A reverential sentiment, which is almost religious in character, connects itself in our minds with the very name of Murray. It is, however, possible to make an injudicious use of these books, and by so doing to miss the fine point of many a pleasure. The very fact that these books are guides to us and invaluable, and that we readily acquire the habit of taking them about with us and consulting them at frequent intervals, comes between us and that rarest and most exquisite enjoyment to be experienced amidst novel scenes. He that visits a place new to him for some special object rightly informs himself of all that the book can tell him. The knowledge may be useful; pleasure is with him a secondary object. But if pleasure be the main object, it will only be experienced in the highest degree by him who goes without book and discovers what old Fuller called the 'observables' for himself. There will be no mental pictures previously formed; consequently what is found will not disappoint. When the mind has been permitted to dwell beforehand on any scene, then, however beautiful or grand it may be, the element of surprise is wanting and admiration is weak. The delight has been discounted.

My own plan, which may be recommended only to those who go out for pleasure – who value happiness above useless (otherwise useful) knowledge, and the pictures that live and glow in memory above albums and collections of photographs – is not to look at a guide-book until the place it treats of has been explored and left behind.

The practical person, to whom this may come as a new idea and who wishes not to waste any time in experiments, would doubtless like to hear how the plan works. He will say that he certainly wants all the happiness to be got out of his rambles, but it is clear that without the book in his pocket he would miss many interesting things: Would the greater degree of pleasure experienced in the others be a sufficient compensation? I should say that he would gain more than he would lose; that vivid interest and pleasure in a few things is preferable to that fainter, more diffused feeling experienced in the other case. Again, we have to take into account the value to us of the mental pictures gathered in our wanderings. For we know that only when a scene is viewed emotionally, when it produces in us a shock of pleasure, does it become a permanent possession of the mind; in other words, it registers an image which, when called up before the inner eye, is capable of reproducing a measure of the original delight.

In recalling those scenes which have given me the greatest happiness, the images of which are most vivid and lasting, I find that most of them are of scenes or objects which were discovered, as it were, by chance, which I had not heard of, or else had heard of and forgotten, or which I had not expected to see. They came as a surprise, and in the following instance one may see that it makes a vast difference whether we do or do not experience such a sensation.

In the course of a ramble on foot in a remote district I came to a small ancient town, set in a cuplike depression amidst high wood-grown hills. The woods were of oak in spring foliage, and against that vivid green I saw the many-gabled tiled roofs and tall chimneys of the old timbered houses, glowing red and warm brown in the brilliant sunshine – a scene of rare beauty, and yet it produced no shock of pleasure; never, in fact, had I looked on a lovely scene for the first time so unemotionally. It seemed to be no new scene, but an old familiar one; and that it had certain degrading associations which took away all delight.

The reason of this was that a great railway company had long been 'booming' this romantic spot, and large photographs, plain and coloured, of the town and its quaint buildings had for years been staring at me in every station and every railway carriage which I had entered on that line. Photography degrades most things, especially open-air things;

3

and in this case, not only had its poor presentments made the scene too familiar, but something of the degradation in the advertising pictures seemed to attach itself to the very scene. Yet even here, after some pleasureless days spent in vain endeavours to shake off these vulgar associations, I was to experience one of the sweetest surprises and delights of my life.

The church of this village-like town is one of its chief attractions; it is a very old and stately building, and its perpendicular tower, nearly a hundred feet high, is one of the noblest in England. It has a magnificent peal of bells, and on a Sunday afternoon they were ringing, filling and flooding that hollow in the hills, seeming to make the houses and trees and the very earth to tremble with the glorious storm of sound. Walking past the church, I followed the streamlet that runs through the town and out by a cleft between the hills to a narrow marshy valley, on the other side of which are precipitous hills, clothed from base to summit in oak woods. As I walked through the cleft the musical roar of the bells followed, and was like a mighty current flowing through and over me; but as I came out the sound from behind ceased suddenly and was now in front, coming back from the hills before me. A sound, but not the same – not a mere echo; and yet an echo it was, the most wonderful I had ever heard. For now that great tempest of musical noise, composed of a multitude of clanging notes with long vibrations, overlapping and mingling and clashing together, seemed at the same time one and many – that tempest from the tower which had mysteriously ceased to be audible came back in strokes or notes distinct and separate and multiplied many times. The sound, the echo, was distributed over the whole face of the steep hill before me, and was changed in character, and it was as if every one of those thousands of oak trees had a peal of bells in it, and that they were raining that far-up bright spiritual tree music down into the valley below. As I stood listening it seemed to me that I had never heard anything so beautiful, nor had any man – not the monk of Eynsham in that vision when he heard the Easter bells on the holy Saturday evening, and described the sound as 'a ringing of a marvellous sweetness, as if all the bells in the world, or whatsoever is of sounding, had been rung together at once.'

Here, then, I had found and had become the possessor of something priceless, since in that moment of surprise and delight the mysterious beautiful sound, with the whole scene, had registered an impression which would outlast all others received at that place, where I had viewed all things with but languid interest. Had it not come as a complete surprise, the emotion experienced and the resultant mental image would not have been so vivid; as it is, I can mentally stand in that valley when I will, seeing that green-wooded hill in front of me and listen to that unearthly music.

Naturally, after quitting the spot, I looked at the first opportunity into a guide-book of the district, only to find that it contained not one word about those wonderful illusive sounds! The book-makers had not done their work well, since it is a pleasure after having discovered something delightful for ourselves to know how others have been affected by it and how they describe it.

Of many other incidents of the kind I will, in this chapter, relate one more, which has a historical or legendary interest. I was staying with the companion of my walks at a village in Southern England in a district new to us. We arrived on a Saturday, and next morning after breakfast went out for a long walk. Turning into the first path across the fields on leaving the village, we came eventually to an oak wood, which was like an open forest, very wild and solitary. In half an hour's walk among the old oaks and underwood we saw no sign of human occupancy, and heard nothing but the woodland birds. We heard, and then saw, the cuckoo for the first time that season, though it was but April the fourth. But the cuckoo was early that spring and had been heard by some from the middle of March. At length, about half-past ten o'clock, we caught sight of a number of people walking in a kind of straggling procession by a path which crossed ours at right angles, headed by a stout old man in a black smock frock and brown leggings, who carried a big book in one hand. One of the processionists we spoke to told us they came from a hamlet a mile away on the borders of the wood and were on their way to church. We elected to follow them, thinking that the church was at some neighbouring village; to our surprise we found it was in the wood, with no other building in sight – a small ancient-looking church built on a raised mound, surrounded by a wide shallow grass-grown trench, on the border of a marshy stream. The people went in and took their seats, while we remained standing just by the door. Then the priest came from the vestry, and seizing the rope vigorously, pulled at it for five minutes, after which he showed us where to sit and the service began. It was very pleasant there, with the door open to the sunlit forest and the little green churchyard without, with a willow wren, the first I had heard, singing his delicate little strain at intervals.

The service over, we rambled an hour longer in the wood, then returned to our village, which had a church of its own, and our landlady, hearing where we had been, told us the story, or tradition, of the little church in the wood. Its origin goes very far back to early Norman times, when all the land in this part was owned by one of William's followers on whom it had been bestowed. He built himself a house or castle on the edge of the forest, where he lived with his wife and two little daughters who were his chief delight. It happened that one day when he was absent the two little girls with their female attendant went into the wood in search of flowers, and that meeting a wild boar they turned and fled, screaming for help. The savage beast pursued, and, quickly overtaking them, attacked the hindermost, the youngest of the two little girls, and killed her, the others escaping in the meantime. On the following day the father returned, and was mad with grief and rage on hearing of the tragedy, and in his madness resolved to go alone on foot to the forest and search for the beast and taste no food or drink until he had slain it. Accordingly to the forest he went, and roamed through it by day and night, and towards the end of the following day he actually found and roused the dreadful animal, and although weakened by his long fast and fatigue, his fury gave him force to fight and conquer it, or else the powers above came to his aid; for when he stood spear in hand to wait the charge of the furious beast he vowed that if he overcame it on that spot he would build a chapel, where God would be worshipped for ever. And there it was raised and has stood to this day, its doors open every Sunday to worshippers, with but one break, some time in the sixteenth century to the third year of Elizabeth, since when there has been no suspension of the weekly service.

That the tradition is not true no one can say. We know that the memory of an action or tragedy of a character to stir the feelings and impress the imagination may live unrecorded in any locality for long centuries. And more, we know or suppose, from at least one quite familiar instance from Flintshire, that a tradition may even take us back to prehistoric times and find corroboration in our own day.

But of this story what corroboration is there, and what do the books say? I have consulted the county history, and no mention is made of such a tradition, and can only assume that the author had never heard it – that he had not the curious Aubrey mind. He only says that it is a very early church – how early he does not know – and adds that it was built 'for the convenience of the inhabitants of the place.' An odd statement, seeing that the place has every appearance of having always been what it is, a forest, and that the inhabitants thereof are weasels, foxes, jays and such-like, and doubtless in former days included wolves, boars, roe-deer and stags, beings which, as Walt Whitman truly remarks, do not worry themselves about their souls.

With this question, however, we need not concern ourselves. To me, after stumbling by chance on the little church in that solitary woodland place, the story of its origin was accepted as true; no doubt it had come down unaltered from generation to generation through all those centuries, and it moved my pity yet was a delight to hear, as great perhaps as it had been to listen to the beautiful chimes many times multiplied from the wooded hill. And if I have a purpose in this book, which is without a purpose, a message to deliver and a lesson to teach, it is only this – the charm of the unknown, and the infinitely greater pleasure in discovering the interesting things for ourselves than in informing ourselves of them by reading. It is like the difference in flavour in wild fruits and all wild meats found and gathered by our own hands in wild places and that of the same prepared and put on the table for us. The ever-varying aspects of nature, of earth and sea and cloud, are a perpetual joy to the artist, who waits and watches for their appearance, who knows that sun and atmosphere have for him revelations without end. They come and go and mock his best efforts; he knows that his striving is in vain – that his weak hands and earthy pigments cannot reproduce these effects or express his feeling – that, as Leighton said, 'every picture is a subject thrown away.' But he has his joy none the less; it is in the pursuit and in the dream of capturing something illusive, mysterious, and inexpressibly beautiful.

CHAPTER TWO

On Going Back

In looking over the preceding chapter it occurred to me that I had omitted something, or rather that it would have been well to drop a word of warning to those who have the desire to revisit a place where they have experienced a delightful surprise. Alas! they cannot have that sensation a second time, and on this account alone the mental image must always be better than its reality. Let the image – the first sharp impression – content us. Many a beautiful picture is spoilt by the artist who cannot be satisfied that he has made the best of his subject, and retouching his canvas to bring out some subtle charm which made the work a success loses it altogether. So in going back, the result of the inevitable disillusionment is that the early mental picture loses something of its original freshness. The very fact that the delightful place or scene was discovered by us made it the shining place it is in memory. And again, the charm we found in it may have been in a measure due to the mood we were in, or to the peculiar aspect in which it came before us at the first, due to the season, to atmospheric and sunlight effects, to some human interest, or to a conjunction of several favourable circumstances; we know we can never see it again in that aspect and with that precise feeling.

On this account I am shy of revisiting the places where I have experienced the keenest delight. For example, I have no desire to revisit that small ancient town among the hills, described in the last chapter; to go on a Sunday evening through that narrow gorge, filled with the musical roar of the church bells; to leave that great sound behind and stand again listening to the marvellous echo from the wooded hill on the other side of the valley. Nor would I care to go again in search of that small ancient lost church in the forest. It would not be early April with the clear sunbeams shining through the old leafless oaks on the floor of fallen yellow leaves with the cuckoo fluting before his time; nor would that straggling procession of villagers appear, headed by an old man in a smock frock with a big book in his hand; nor would I hear for the first time the strange history of the church which so enchanted me.

I will here give an account of yet another of the many well-remembered delightful spots which I would not revisit, nor even look upon again if I could avoid doing so by going several miles out of my way.

It was green open country in the west of England – very far west, although on the east side of the Tamar – in a beautiful spot remote from railroads and large towns, and the road by which I was travelling (on this occasion on a bicycle) ran or serpentined along the foot of a range of low round hills on my right hand, while on my left I had a green valley with other low round green hills beyond it. The valley had a marshy stream with sedgy margins and occasional clumps of alder and willow trees. It was the end of a hot midsummer day; the sun went down a vast globe of crimson fire in a crystal clear sky; and as I was going east I was obliged to dismount and stand still to watch its setting. When the great red disc had gone down behind the green world I resumed my way but went slowly, then slower still, the better to enjoy the delicious coolness which came from the moist valley and the beauty of the evening in that solitary place which I had never looked on before. Nor was there any need to hurry; I had but three or four miles to go to the small old town where I intended passing the night. By and by the winding road led me down close to the stream at a point where it broadened to a large still pool. This was the ford, and on the other side was a small rustic village, consisting of a church, two or three farm-houses with their barns and outbuildings, and a few ancient-looking stone cottages with thatched roofs. But the church was the main thing; it was a noble building with a very fine tower, and from its size and beauty I concluded that it was an ancient church dating back to the time when there was a passion in the West Country and in many parts of England of building these great fanes even in the remotest and most thinly populated parishes. In this I was mistaken through having seen it at a distance from the other side of the ford after the sun had set.

Never, I thought, had I seen a lovelier village with its old picturesque cottages shaded by ancient oaks and elms, and the great church with its stately tower looking dark against the luminous western sky. Dismounting again I stood for some time admiring the scene, wishing that I could make that village my home for the rest of my life, conscious at the same time that it was the mood, the season, the magical hour which made it seem so enchanting. Presently a young man, the first human figure that presented itself to my sight, appeared, mounted on a big carthorse and leading a second horse by a halter, and rode down into the pool to bathe the animals' legs and give them a drink. He was a sturdy-looking young fellow with a sun-browned face, in earth-coloured, working clothes, with a small cap stuck on the back of his round curly head; he probably imagined himself not a bad-looking young man, for while his horses were drinking he laid over on the broad bare backs and bending down studied his own reflection in the bright water. Then an old woman came out of a cottage close by, and began talking to him in her West Country dialect in a thin high-pitched cracked voice. Their talking was the only sound in the village; so silent was it that all the rest of its inhabitants might have been in bed and fast asleep; then, the conversation ended, the young man rode out with a great splashing and the old woman turned into her cottage again, and I was left in solitude.

Still I lingered: I could not go just yet; the chances were that I should never again see that sweet village in that beautiful aspect at the twilight hour.

For now it came into my mind that I could not very well settle there for the rest of my life; I could not, in fact, tie myself to any place without sacrificing certain other advantages I possessed; and the main thing was that by taking root I should deprive myself of the chance of looking on still other beautiful scenes and experiencing other sweet surprises. I was wishing that I had come a little earlier on the scene to have had time to borrow the key of the church and get a sight of the interior, when all at once I heard a shrill voice and a boy appeared running across the wide green space of the churchyard. A second boy followed, then another, then still others, and I saw that they were going into the church by the side door. They were choir-boys going to practice. The church was open then, and late as it was I could have half an hour inside before it was dark! The stream was spanned by an old stone bridge above the ford, and going over it I at once made my way to the great building, but even before entering it I discovered that it possessed an organ of extraordinary power and that someone was performing on it with a vengeance. Inside the noise was tremendous – a bigger noise from an organ, it seemed to me, than I had ever heard before, even at the Albert Hall and the Crystal Palace, but even more astonishing than the uproar was the sight that met my eyes. The boys, nine or ten sturdy little rustics with round sunburnt West Country faces, were playing the roughest game ever witnessed in a church. Some were engaged in a sort of flying fight, madly pursuing one another up and down the aisles and over the pews, and whenever one overtook another he would seize hold of him and they would struggle together until one was thrown and received a vigorous pommelling. Those who were not fighting were dancing to the music. It was great fun to them, and they were shouting and laughing their loudest only not a sound of it all could be heard on account of the thunderous roar of the organ which filled and seemed to make the whole building tremble. The boys took no notice of me, and seeing that there was a singularly fine west window, I went to it and stood there some time with my back to the game which was going on at the other end of the building, admiring the beautiful colours and trying to make out the subjects depicted. In the centre part, lit by the after-glow in the sky to a wonderful brilliance, was the figure of a saint, a lovely young woman in a blue robe with an abundance of loose golden-red hair and an aureole about her head. Her pale face wore a sweet and placid expression, and her eyes of a pure forget-me-not blue were looking straight into mine. As I stood there the music, or noise, ceased and a very profound silence followed – not a giggle, not a whisper from the outrageous young barbarians, and not a sound of the organist or of anyone speaking to them. Presently I became conscious of some person standing almost but not quite abreast of me, and turning sharply I found a clergyman at my side. He was the vicar, the person who had been letting himself go on the organ; a slight man with a handsome, pale, ascetic face, clean-shaven, very dark-eyed, looking more like an Italian monk or priest than an English clergyman. But although rigidly ecclesiastic in his appearance and dress, there was something curiously engaging in him, along with a subtle look which it was not easy to fathom. There was a light in his dark eyes which reminded me of a flame seen through a smoked glass or a thin black veil, and a slight restless movement about the corners of his mouth as if a smile was just on the point of breaking out. But it never quite came; he kept his gravity even when he said things which would have gone very well with a smile.

'I see,' he spoke, and his penetrating musical voice had, too, like his eyes and mouth, an expression of mystery in it, 'that you are admiring our beautiful west window, especially the figure in the centre. It is quite new – everything is new here – the church itself was only built a few years ago. This window is its chief glory: it was done by a good artist – he has done some of the most admired windows of recent years; and the centre figure is supposed to be a portrait of our generous patroness. At all events she sat for it to him. You have probably heard of Lady Y—?'

11

'What!' I exclaimed. 'Lady Y—: that funny old woman!'

'No – middle-aged,' he corrected, a little frigidly and perhaps a little mockingly at the same time.

'Very well, middle-aged if you like; I don't know her personally. One hears about her; but I did not know she had a place in these parts.'

'She owns most of this parish and has done so much for us that we can very well look leniently on a little weakness – her wish that the future inhabitants of the place shall not remember her as a middle-aged woman not remarkable for good looks – 'funny,' as you just now said.'

He was wonderfully candid, I thought. But what extraordinary benefits had she bestowed on them, I asked, to enable them to regard, or to say, that this picture of a very beautiful young female was her likeness!

'Why,' he said, 'the church would not have been built but for her. We were astonished at the sum she offered to contribute towards the work, and at once set about pulling the small old church down so as to rebuild on the exact site.'

'Do you know,' I returned, 'I can't help saying something you will not like to hear. It is a very fine church, no doubt, but it always angers me to hear of a case like this where some ancient church is pulled down and a grand new one raised in its place to the honour and glory of some rich parvenu with or without a brand new title.'

'You are not hurting me in the least,' he replied, with that change which came from time to time in his eyes as if the flame behind the screen had suddenly grown brighter. 'I agree with every word you say; the meanest church in the land should be cherished as long as it will hold together. But unfortunately ours had to come down. It was very old and decayed past mending. The floor was six feet below the level of the surrounding ground and frightfully damp. It had been examined over and over again by experts during the past forty or fifty years, and from the first they pronounced it a hopeless case, so that it was never restored. The interior, right down to the time of demolition, was like that of most country churches of a century ago, with the old black worm-eaten pews, in which the worshippers shut themselves up as if in their own houses or castles. On account of the damp we were haunted by toads. You smile, sir, but it was no smiling matter for me during my first year as vicar, when I discovered that it was the custom here to keep pet toads in the church. It sounds strange and funny, no doubt, but it is a fact that all the best people in the parish had one of these creatures, and it was customary for the ladies to bring it a weekly supply of provisions – bits of meat, hard-boiled eggs chopped up, and earth-worms, and whatever else they fancied it would like – in their reticules. The toads, I suppose, knew when it was Sunday – their feeding day; at all events they would crawl out of their holes in the floor under the pews to receive their rations – and caresses. The toads got on my nerves with rather unpleasant consequences. I preached in a way which my listeners did not appreciate or properly understand, particularly when I took for my subject our duty towards the lower animals, including reptiles.'

'Batrachians,' I interposed, echoing as well as I could the tone in which he had rebuked me before.

'Very well, batrachians – I am not a naturalist. But the impression created on their minds appeared to be that I was rather an odd person in the pulpit. When the time came to pull the old church down the toad-keepers were bidden to remove their pets, which they did with considerable reluctance. What became of them I do not know – I never inquired. I used to have a careful inspection made of the floor to make sure that these creatures were not put back in the new building, and I am happy to think it is not suited to their habits. The floors are very well cemented, and are dry and clean.'

Having finished his story he invited me to go to the parsonage and get some refreshment. 'I daresay you are thirsty,' he said.

But it was getting late; it was almost dark in the church by now, although the figure of the golden-haired saint still glowed in the window and gazed at us out of her blue eyes. 'I must not waste more of your time,' I added. 'There are your boys still patiently waiting to begin their practice – such nice quiet fellows!'

'Yes, they are,' he returned a little bitterly, a sudden accent of weariness in his voice and no trace now of what I had seen in his countenance a little while ago – the light that shone and brightened behind the dark eye and the little play about the corners of the mouth as of dimpling motions on the surface of a pool.

And in that new guise, or disguise, I left him, the austere priest with nothing to suggest the whimsical or grotesque in his cold ascetic face. Recrossing the bridge I stood a little time and looked once more at the noble church tower standing dark against the clear amber-coloured sky, and said to myself: 'Why, this is one of the oddest incidents of my life! Not that I have seen or heard anything very wonderful – just a small rustic village, one of a thousand in the land; a big new church in which some person was playing rather madly on the organ, a set of unruly choir-boys; a handsome stained-glass west window, and, finally, a nice little chat with the vicar.' It was not in these things; it was a sense of something strange in the mind, of something in some way unlike all other places and people and experiences. The sensation was like that of the reader who becomes absorbed in Henry Newbolt's romance of *The Old Country*, who identifies himself with the hero and unconsciously, or without quite knowing how, slips back out of this modern world into that of half a thousand years ago. It is the same familiar green land in which he finds himself – the same old country and the same sort of people with feelings and habits of life and thought unchangeable as the colour of grass and flowers, the songs of birds and the smell of the earth, yet with a difference. I recognized it chiefly in the parish priest I had been conversing with; for one thing, his mediaeval mind evidently did not regard a sense of humour and of the grotesque as out of place in or on a sacred building. If it had been lighter I should have looked at the roof for an effigy of a semi-human toad-like creature smiling down mockingly at the worshippers as they came and went.

On departing it struck me that it would assuredly be a mistake to return to this village and look at it again by the common lights of day. No, it was better to keep the impressions I had gathered unspoilt; even to believe, if I could, that no such place existed, but that it had existed exactly as I had found it, even to the unruly choir-boys, the ascetic-looking priest with a strange light in his eyes, and the worshippers who kept pet toads in the church. They were not precisely like people of the twentieth century. As for the eccentric middle-aged or elderly person whose portrait adorned the west window, she was not the lady I knew something about, but another older Lady Y – , who flourished some six or seven centuries ago.

CHAPTER THREE

Walking and Cycling

We know that there cannot be progression without retrogression, or gain with no corresponding loss; and often on my wheel, when flying along the roads at a reckless rate of very nearly nine miles an hour, I have regretted that time of limitations, galling to me then, when I was compelled to go on foot. I am a walker still, but with other means of getting about I do not feel so native to the earth as formerly. That is a loss. Yet a poorer walker it would have been hard to find, and on even my most prolonged wanderings the end of each day usually brought extreme fatigue. This, too, although my only companion was slow – slower than the poor proverbial snail or tortoise – and I would leave her half a mile or so behind to force my way through unkept hedges, climb hills, and explore woods and thickets to converse with every bird and shy little beast and scaly creature I could discover. But mark what follows. In the late afternoon I would be back in the road or footpath, satisfied to go slow, then slower still, until – the snail in woman shape would be obliged to slacken her pace to keep me company, and even to stand still at intervals to give me needful rest.

But there were compensations, and one, perhaps the best of all, was that this method of seeing the country made us more intimate with the people we met and stayed with. They were mostly poor people, cottagers in small remote villages; and we, too, were poor, often footsore, in need of their ministrations, and nearer to them on that account than if we had travelled in a more comfortable way. I can recall a hundred little adventures we met with during those wanderings, when we walked day after day, without map or guide-book as our custom was, not knowing where the evening would find us, but always confident that the people to whom it would fall in the end to shelter us would prove interesting to know and would show us a kindness that money could not pay for. Of these hundred little incidents let me relate one.

It was near the end of a long summer day when we arrived at a small hamlet of about a dozen cottages on the edge of an extensive wood – a forest it is called; and, coming to it, we said that here we *must* stay, even if we had to spend the night sitting in a porch. The men and women we talked to all assured us that they did not know of anyone who could take us in, but there was Mr. Brownjohn, who kept the shop, and was the right person to apply to. Accordingly we went to the little general shop and heard that Mr. Brownjohn was not at home. His housekeeper, a fat, dark, voluble woman with prominent black eyes, who minded the shop in the master's absence, told us that Mr. Brownjohn had gone to a neighbouring farm-house on important business, but was expected back shortly. We waited, and by and by he returned, a shabbily dressed, weak-looking little old man, with pale blue eyes and thin yellowish white hair. He could not put us up, he said, he had no room in his cottage; there was nothing for us but to go on to the next place, a village three miles distant, on the chance of finding a bed there. We assured him that we could go no further, and after revolving the matter a while longer he again said that we could not stay, as there was not a room to be had in the place since poor Mrs. Flowerdew had her trouble. She had a spare room and used to take in a lodger occasionally, and a good handy woman she was too; but now – no, Mrs. Flowerdew could not take us in. We questioned him, and he said that no one had died there and there had been no illness. They were all quite well at Mrs. Flowerdew's; the trouble was of another kind. There was no more to be said about it.

As nothing further could be got out of him we went in search of Mrs. Flowerdew herself, and found her in a pretty vine-clad cottage. She was a young woman, very poorly dressed, with a pleasing but careworn face, and she had four small, bright, healthy, happy-faced children. They were all grouped round her as she stood in the doorway to speak to us, and they too were poorly dressed and poorly shod. When we told our tale she appeared ready to burst into tears. Oh, how unfortunate it was that she could not take us in! It would have made her so happy, and the few shillings would have been such a blessing! But what could she do now – the landlord's agent had put in a distress and carried off and sold all her best things. Every stick out of her nice spare room had been taken from them! Oh, it was cruel!

As we wished to hear more she told us the whole story. They had got behindhand with the rent, but that had often been the case, only this time it happened that the agent wanted a cottage for a person he wished to befriend, and so gave them notice to quit. But her husband was a high-spirited man and determined to stick to his rights, so he informed the agent that he refused to move until he received compensation for his improvements.

Questioned about these improvements, she led us through to the back to show us the ground, about half an acre in extent, part of which was used as a paddock for the donkey, and on the other part there were about a dozen rather sickly-looking young fruit trees. Her husband, she said, had planted the orchard and kept the fence of the paddock in order, and they refused to compensate him! Then she took us up to the spare room, empty of furniture, the floor thick with dust. The bed, table, chairs, washhandstand, toilet service – the things she had been so long struggling to get together, saving her money for months and months, and making so many journeys to the town to buy – all, all he had taken away and sold for almost nothing!

Then, actually with tears in her eyes, she said that now we knew why she couldn't take us in – why she had to seem so unkind.

But we are going to stay, we told her. It was a very good room; she could surely get a few things to put in it, and in the meantime we would go and forage for provisions to last us till Monday.

It is odd to find how easy it is to get what one wants by simply taking it! At first she was amazed at our decision, then she was delighted and said she would go out to her neighbours and try to borrow all that was wanted in the way of furniture and bedding. Then we returned to Mr. Brownjohn's to buy bread, bacon, and groceries, and he in turn sent us to Mr. Marling for vegetables. Mr. Marling heard us, and soberly taking up a spade and other implements led us out to his garden and dug us a mess of potatoes while we waited. In the meantime good Mrs. Flowerdew had not been idle, and we formed the idea that her neighbours must have been her debtors for unnumbered little kindnesses, so eager did they now appear to do her a good turn. Out of one cottage a woman was seen coming burdened with a big roll of bedding; from others children issued bearing cane chairs, basin and ewer, and so on, and when we next looked into our room we found it swept and scrubbed, mats on the floor, and quite comfortably furnished.

After our meal in the small parlour, which had been given up to us, the family having migrated into the kitchen, we sat for an hour by the open window looking out on the dim forest and saw the moon rise – a great golden globe above the trees – and listened to the reeling of the nightjars. So many were the birds, reeling on all sides, at various distances, that the evening air seemed full of their sounds, far and near, like many low, tremulous, sustained notes blown on reeds, rising and falling, overlapping and mingling. And presently from the bushes close by, just beyond the weedy, forlorn little 'orchard,' sounded the rich, full, throbbing prelude to the nightingale's song, and that powerful melody that in its purity and brilliance invariably strikes us with surprise seemed to shine out, as it were, against the background of that diffused, mysterious purring of the nightjars, even as the golden disc of the moon shone against and above the darkening skies and dusky woods.

And as we sat there, gazing and listening, a human voice came out of the night – a call prolonged and modulated like the coo-ee of the Australian bush, far off and faint; but the children in the kitchen heard it at the same time, for they too had been listening, and instantly went mad with excitement.

'Father!' they all screamed together. 'Father's coming!' and out they rushed and away they fled down the darkening road, exerting their four voices in shrill answering cries.

We were anxious to see this unfortunate man, who was yet happy in a loving family. He had gone early in the morning in his donkey-cart to the little market town, fourteen miles away, to get the few necessaries they could afford to buy. Doubtless they would be very few. We had not long to wait, as the white donkey that drew the cart had put on a tremendous spurt at the end, notwithstanding that the four youngsters had climbed in to add to his burden. But what was our surprise to behold in the charioteer a tall, gaunt, grey-faced old man with long white hair and beard! He must have been seventy, that old man with a young wife and four happy bright-eyed little children!

We could understand it better when he finally settled down in his corner in the kitchen and began to relate the events of the day, addressing his poor little wife, now busy darning or patching an old garment, while the children, clustered at his knee, listened as to a fairy tale. Certainly this white-haired man had not grown old in mind; he was keenly interested in all he saw and heard, and he had seen and heard much in the little market town that day. Cattle and pigs and sheep and shepherds and sheepdogs; farmers, shopkeepers, dealers, publicans, tramps, and gentlefolks in carriages and on horseback; shops, too, with beautiful new things in the windows; millinery, agricultural implements, flowers and fruit and vegetables; toys and books and sweeties of all colours. And the people he had met on the road and at market, and what they had said to him about the weather and their business and the prospects of the year, how their wives and children were, and the clever jokes they had made, and his own jokes, which were the cleverest of all. If he had just returned from Central Africa or from Thibet he could not have had more to tell them nor told it with greater zest.

We went to our room, but until the small hours the wind of the old traveller's talk could still be heard at intervals from the kitchen, mingled with occasional shrill explosions of laughter from the listening children.

It happened that on the following day, spent in idling in the forest and about the hamlet, conversing with the cottagers, we were told that our old man was a bit of a humbug; that he was a great talker, with a hundred schemes for the improvement of his fortunes, and, incidently, for the benefit of his neighbours and the world at large; but nothing came of it all and he was now fast sinking into the lowest depths of poverty. Yet who would blame him? 'Tis the nature of the gorse to be 'unprofitably gay.' All that, however, is a question for the moralist; the point now is that in walking, even in that poor way, when, on account of physical weakness, it was often a pain and weariness, there are alleviations which may be more to us than positive pleasures, and scenes to delight the eye that are missed by the wheelman in his haste, or but dimly seen or vaguely surmised in passing – green refreshing nooks and crystal streamlets, and shadowy woodland depths with glimpses of a blue sky beyond – all in the wilderness of the human heart.

CHAPTER FOUR

Seeking a Shelter

The 'walks' already spoken of, at a time when life had little or no other pleasure for us on account of poverty and ill-health, were taken at pretty regular intervals two or three times a year. It all depended on our means; in very lean years there was but one outing. It was impossible to escape altogether from the immense unfriendly wilderness of London simply because, albeit 'unfriendly,' it yet appeared to be the only place in the wide world where our poor little talents could earn us a few shillings a week to live on. Music and literature! but I fancy the nearest crossing-sweeper did better, and could afford to give himself a more generous dinner every day. It occasionally happened that an article sent to some magazine was not returned, and always after so many rejections to have one accepted and paid for with a cheque worth several pounds was a cause of astonishment, and was as truly a miracle as if the angel of the sun had compassionately thrown us down a handful of gold. And out of these little handfuls enough was sometimes saved for the country rambles at Easter and Whitsuntide and in the autumn. It was during one of these Easter walks, when seeking for a resting-place for the night, that we met with another adventure worth telling.

We had got to that best part of Surrey not yet colonized by wealthy men from the City, but where all things are as they were of old, when, late in the day, we came to a pleasant straggling village with one street a mile long. Here we resolved to stay, and walked the length of the street making inquiries, but were told by every person we spoke to that the only place we could stay at was the inn – the 'White Hart.' When we said we preferred to stay at a cottage they smiled a pitying smile. No, there was no such place. But we were determined not to go to the inn, although it had a very inviting look, and was well placed with no other house near it, looking on the wide village green with ancient trees shading the road on either side.

Having passed it and got to the end of the village, we turned and walked back, still making vain inquiries, passing it again, and when once more at the starting-point we were in despair when we spied a man coming along the middle of the road and went out to meet him to ask the weary question for the last time. His appearance was rather odd as he came towards us on that blowy March evening with dust and straws flying past and the level sun shining full on him. He was tall and slim, with a large round smooth face and big pale-blue innocent-looking eyes, and he walked rapidly but in a peculiar jerky yet shambling manner, swinging and tossing his legs and arms about. Moving along in this disjointed manner in his loose fluttering clothes he put one in mind of a big flimsy newspaper blown along the road by the wind.

This unpromising-looking person at once told us that there *was* a place where we could stay; he knew it well, for it happened to be his father's house and his own home. It was away at the other end of the village. His people had given accommodation to strangers before, and would be glad to receive us and make us comfortable.

Surprised, and a little doubtful of our good fortune, I asked my young man if he could explain the fact that so many of his neighbours had assured us that no accommodation was to be had in the village except at the inn. He did not make a direct reply. He said that the ways of the villagers were not the ways of his people. He and all his house cherished only kind feelings towards their neighbours; whether those feelings were returned or not, it was not for him to say. And there was something else. A small appointment which would keep a man from want for the term of his natural life, without absorbing all his time, had become vacant in the village. Several of the young men in the place were anxious to have it; then he, too, came forward as a candidate, and all the others jeered at him and tried to laugh him out of it. He cared nothing for that, and when the examination came off he proved the best man and got the place. He had fought his fight and had overcome all his enemies; if they did not like him any the better for his victory, and did and said little things to injure him, he did not mind much, he could afford to forgive them.

Having finished his story, he said good-bye, and went his way, blown, as it were, along the road by the wind.

We were now very curious to see the other members of his family; they would, we imagined, prove amusing, if nothing better. They proved a good deal better. The house we sought, for a house it was, stood a little way back from the street in a large garden. It had in former times been an inn, or farm-house, possibly a manor-house, and was large, with many small rooms, and short, narrow, crooked staircases, half-landings and narrow passages, and a few large rooms, their low ceilings resting on old oak beams, black as ebony. Outside, it was the most picturesque and doubtless the oldest house in the village; many-gabled, with very tall ancient chimneys, the roofs of red tiles mottled grey and yellow with age and lichen. It was a surprise to find a woodman – for that was what the man was – living in such a big place. The woodman himself, his appearance and character, gave us a second and greater surprise. He was a well-shaped man of medium height; although past middle life he looked young, and had no white thread in his raven-black hair and beard. His teeth were white and even, and his features as perfect as I have seen in any man. His eyes were pure dark blue, contrasting rather strangely with his pale olive skin and intense black hair. Only a woodman, but he might have come of one of the oldest and best families in the country, if there is any connection between good blood and fine features and a noble expression. Oddly enough, his surname was an uncommon and aristocratic one. His wife, on the other hand, although a very good woman as we found, had a distinctly plebeian countenance. One day she informed us that she came of a different and better class than her husband's. She was the daughter of a small tradesman, and had begun life as a lady's-maid: her husband was nothing but a labourer; his people had been labourers for generations, consequently her marriage to him had involved a considerable descent in the social scale. Hearing this, it was hard to repress a smile.

The contrast between this man and the ordinary villager of his class was as great in manners and conversation as in features and expression. His combined dignity and gentleness, and apparent unconsciousness of any caste differences between man and man, were astonishing in one who had been a simple toiler all his life.

There were some grown-up children, others growing up, with others that were still quite small. The boys, I noticed, favoured their mother, and had commonplace faces; the girls took after their father, and though their features were not so perfect they were exceptionally good-looking. The eldest son – the disjointed, fly-away-looking young man who had conquered all his enemies – had a wife and child. The eldest daughter was also married, and had one child. Altogether the three families numbered about sixteen persons, each family having its separate set of rooms, but all dining at one table. How did they do it? It seemed easy enough to them. They were serious people in a sense, although always cheerful and sometimes hilarious when together of an evening, or at

their meals. But they regarded life as a serious matter, a state of proba-
tion; they were non-smokers, total abstainers, diligent at their work,
united, profoundly religious. A fresh wonder came to light when I found
that this poor woodman, with so large a family to support, who spent
ten or twelve hours every day at his outdoor work, had yet been able
out of his small earnings to buy bricks and other materials, and, assisted
by his sons, to build a chapel adjoining his house. Here he held religious services on Sundays, and once or twice of an evening during the
week. These services consisted of extempore prayers, a short address,
and hymns accompanied by a harmonium, which they all appeared able
to play.

What his particular doctrine was I did not inquire, nor did I wish for
any information on that point. Doubtless he was a dissenter of some
kind living in a village where there was no chapel; the services were
for the family, but were also attended by a few of the villagers and
some persons from neighbouring farms who preferred a simpler form
of worship to that of the Church.

It was not strange that this little community should have been
regarded with something like disfavour by the other villagers. For these
others, man for man, made just as much money, and paid less rent for
their small cottages, and, furthermore, received doles from the vicar
and his well-to-do parishioners, yet they could not better their position,
much less afford the good clothing, books, music, and other pleasant
things which the independent woodman bestowed on his family. And
they knew why. The woodman's very presence in their midst was a continual reproach, a sermon on improvidence and intemperance, which
they could not avoid hearing by thrusting their fingers into their ears.

During my stay with these people something occurred to cause them
a very deep disquiet. The reader will probably smile when I tell them
what it was. Awaking one night after midnight I heard the unusual
sound of voices in earnest conversation in the room below; this went
on until I fell asleep again. In the morning we noticed that our landlady
had a somewhat haggard face, and that the daughters also had pale
faces, with purple marks under the eyes, as if they had kept their mother
company in some sorrowful vigil. We were not left long in ignorance of
the cause of this cloud. The good woman asked if we had been much
disturbed by the talking. I answered that I had heard voices and had
supposed that friends from a distance had arrived overnight and that

they had sat up talking to a late hour. No – that was not it, she said; but someone had arrived late, a son who was sixteen years old, and who had been absent for some days on a visit to relations in another county. When they gathered round him to hear his news he confessed that while away he had learnt to smoke, and he now wished them to know that he had well considered the matter, and was convinced that it was not wrong nor harmful to smoke, and was determined not to give up his tobacco. They had talked to him – father, mother, brothers, and sisters – using every argument they could find or invent to move him, until it was day and time for the woodman to go to his woods, and the others to their several occupations. But their 'all-night sitting' had been wasted; the stubborn youth had not been convinced nor shaken. When, after morning prayers, they got up from their knees, the sun-light shining in upon them, they had made a last appeal with tears in their eyes, and he had refused to give the promise they asked. The poor woman was greatly distressed. This young fellow, I thought, favours his mother in features, but mentally he is perhaps more like his father. Being a smoker myself I ventured to put in a word for him. They were distressing themselves too much, I told her; smoking in moderation was not only harmless, especially to those who worked out of doors, but it was a well-nigh universal habit, and many leading men in the religious world, both churchmen and dissenters, were known to be smokers.

Her answer, which came quickly enough, was that they did not regard the practice of smoking as in itself bad, but they knew that in some circumstances it was inexpedient; and in the case of her son they were troubled at the thought of what smoking would ultimately lead to. People, she continued, did not care to smoke, any more than they did to eat and drink, in solitude. It was a social habit, and it was inevitable that her boy should look for others to keep him company in smoking. There would be no harm in that in the summer-time when young people like to keep out of doors until bedtime; but during the long winter evenings he would have to look for his companions in the parlour of the public-house. And it would not be easy, scarcely possible, to sit long among the others without drinking a little beer. It is really no more wrong to drink a little beer than to smoke, he would say; and it would be true. One pipe would lead to another and one glass of beer to another. The habit would be formed and at last all his evenings and all his earnings would be spent in the public-house.

She was right, and I had nothing more to say except to wish her success in her efforts.

It is curious that the strongest protests against the evils of the village public, which one hears from village women, come from those who are not themselves sufferers. Perhaps it is not curious. Instinctively we hide our sores, bodily and mental, from the public gaze.

Not long ago I was in a small rustic village in Wiltshire, perhaps the most charming village I have seen in that county. There was no inn or ale-house, and feeling very thirsty after my long walk I went to a cottage and asked the woman I saw there for a drink of milk. She invited me in, and spreading a clean cloth on the table, placed a jug of new milk, a loaf, and butter before me. For these good things she proudly refused to accept payment. As she was a handsome young woman, with a clear, pleasant voice, I was glad to have her sit there and talk to me while I refreshed myself. Besides, I was in search of information and got it from her during our talk. My object in going to the village was to see a woman who, I had been told, was living there. I now heard that her cottage was close by, but unfortunately, while anxious to see her, I had no excuse for calling.

'Do you think,' said I to my young hostess, 'that it would do to tell her that I had heard something of her strange history and misfortunes, and wished to offer her a little help? Is she very poor?'

'Oh, no,' she replied. 'Please do not offer her money, if you see her. She would be offended. There is no one in this village who would take a shilling as a gift from a stranger. We all have enough; there is not a poor person among us.'

'What a happy village!' I exclaimed. 'Perhaps you are all total abstainers.'

She laughed, and said that they all brewed their own beer – there was not a total abstainer among them. Every cottager made from fifty to eighty gallons, or more, and they drank beer every day, but very moderately, while it lasted. They were all very sober; their children would have to go to some neighbouring village to see a tipsy man.

I remarked that at the next village, which had three public-houses, there were a good many persons so poor that they would gladly at any time take a shilling from any-one.

It was the same everywhere in the district, she said, except in that village which had no public-house. Not only were they better off, and independent of blanket societies and charity in all forms, but they were infinitely happier. And after the day's work the men came home to spend the evening with their wives and children.

At this stage I was surprised by a sudden burst of passion on her part. She stood up, her face flushing red, and solemnly declared that if ever a public-house was opened in that village, and if the men took to spending their evenings in it, her husband with them, she would not endure such a condition of things – she wondered that so many women endured it – but would take her little ones and go away to earn her own living under some other roof.

CHAPTER FIVE

Wind, Wave and Spirit

The rambles I have described were mostly inland: when by chance they took us down to the sea our impressions and adventures appeared less interesting. Looking back on the holiday, it would seem to us a somewhat vacant time compared to one spent in wandering from village to village. I mean if we do not take into account that first impression which the sea invariably makes on us on returning to it after a long absence – the shock of recognition and wonder and joy as if we had been suffering from loss of memory and it had now suddenly come back to us. That brief moving experience over, there is little the sea can give us to compare with the land. How could it be otherwise in our case, seeing that we were by it in a crowd, our movements and way of life regulated for us in places which appear like overgrown and ill-organized convalescent homes? There was always a secret intense dislike of all parasitic and holiday places, an uncomfortable feeling which made the pleasure seem poor and the remembrance of days so spent hardly worth dwelling on. And as we are able to keep in or throw out of our minds whatever we please, being autocrats in our own little kingdom, I elected to cast away most of the memories of these comparatively insipid holidays. But not all, and of those I retain I will describe at least two, one in the present chapter on the East Anglian coast, the other later on.

It was cold, though the month was August; it blew and the sky was grey and rain beginning to fall when we came down about noon to a small town on the Norfolk coast, where we hoped to find lodging and such comforts as could be purchased out of a slender purse. It was a small modern pleasure town of an almost startling appearance owing to the material used in building its straight rows of cottages and its ugly square houses and villas. This was an orange-brown stone found in the neighbourhood, the roofs being all of hard, black slate. I had never seen houses of such a colour, it was stronger, more glaring and aggressive than the reddest brick, and there was not a green thing to partially screen or soften it, nor did the darkness of the wet weather have any mitigating effect on it. The town was built on high ground, with an open grassy space before it sloping down to the cliff in which steps had been cut to give access to the beach, and beyond the cliff we caught sight of the grey, desolate, wind-vexed sea. But the rain was coming down more and more heavily, turning the streets into torrents, so that we began to envy those who had found a shelter even in so ugly a place. No one would take us in. House after house, street after street, we tried, and at every door with '*Apartments to Let*' over it where we knocked the same hateful landlady-face appeared with the same triumphant gleam in the fish-eyes and the same smile on the mouth that opened to tell us delightedly that she and the town were 'full up'; that never had there been known such a rush of visitors; applicants were being turned away every hour from every door!

After three miserable hours spent in this way we began inquiring at all the shops, and eventually at one were told of a poor woman in a small house in a street a good way back from the front who would perhaps be able to taken us in. To this place we went and knocked at a low door in a long blank wall in a narrow street; it was opened to us by a pale thin sad-looking woman in a rusty black gown, who asked us into a shabby parlour, and agreed to take us in until we could find something better. She had a gentle voice and was full of sympathy, and seeing our plight took us into the kitchen behind the parlour, which was living- and working-room as well, to dry ourselves by the fire.

'The greatest pleasure in life,' said once a magnificent young athlete, a great pedestrian, to me, 'is to rest when you are tired.' And, I should add, to dry and warm yourself by a big fire when wet and cold, and to eat and drink when you are hungry and thirsty. All these pleasures were now ours, for very soon tea and chops were ready for us; and so strangely human, so sister-like did this quiet helpful woman seem after our harsh experiences on that rough rainy day – that we congratulated ourselves on our good fortune in having found such a haven, and soon informed her that we wanted no 'better place.'

She worked with her needle to support herself and her one child, a little boy of ten; and by and by when he came in pretty wet from some outdoor occupation we made his acquaintance and the discovery that he was a little boy of an original character. He was so much to his mother, who, poor soul, had nobody else in the world to love, that she was always haunted by the fear of losing him. He was her boy, the child of her body, exclusively her own, unlike all other boys, and her wise heart told her that if she put him in a school he would be changed so that she would no longer know him for her boy. For it is true that our schools are factories, with a machinery to unmake and remake, or fabricate, the souls of children much in the way in which shoddy is manufactured. You may see a thousand rags or garments of a thousand shapes and colours cast in to be boiled, bleached, pulled to pieces, combed and woven, and finally come out as a piece of cloth a thousand yards long of a uniform harmonious pattern, smooth, glossy, and respectable. His individuality gone, he would in a sense be lost to her; and although by nature a weak timid woman, though poor, and a stranger in a strange place, this thought, or feeling, or 'ridiculous delusion' as most people would call it, had made her strong, and she had succeeded in keeping her boy out of school.

Hers was an interesting story. Left alone in the world she had married one in her own class, very happily as she imagined. He was in some business in a country town, well off enough to provide a comfortable home, and he was very good; in fact, his one fault was that he was too good, too open-hearted and fond of associating with other good fellows like himself, and of pledging them in the cup that cheers and at the same time inebriates. Nevertheless, things went very well for a time, until the child was born, the business declined, and they began to be a little pinched. Then it occurred to her that she, too, might be able to do something. She started dressmaking, and as she had good taste and was clever and quick, her business soon prospered. This pleased him; it relieved him from the necessity of providing for the home, and enabled him to follow his own inclination, which was to take things easily – to be an idle man, with a little ready money in his pocket for betting and other pleasures. The money was now provided out of 'our business.' This state of things continued without any change, except that process of degeneration which continued in him, until the child was about four years old, when all at once one day he told her they were not doing as well as they might. She was giving far too much of her time and attention to domestic matters – to the child especially. Business was business – a thing it was hard for a woman to understand – and it was impossible for her to give her mind properly to it with her thoughts occupied with the child. It couldn't be done. Let the child be put away, he said, and the receipts would probably be doubled. He had been making inquiries and found that for a modest annual payment the boy could be taken proper care of at a distance by good decent people he had heard of.

She had never suspected such a thought in his mind, and this proposal had the effect of a stunning blow. She answered not one word: he said his say and went out, and she knew she would not see him again for many hours, perhaps not for some days; she knew, too, that he would say no more to her on the subject, that it would all be arranged about the child with or without her consent. His will was law, her wishes nothing. For she was his wife and humble obedient slave; never had she pleaded with or admonished him and never complained, even when, after her long day of hard work, he came in at ten or eleven o'clock at night with several of his pals, all excited with drink and noisy as himself, to call for supper. Nevertheless she had been happy – intensely happy, because of the child. The love for the man she had married, wondering how one so bright and handsome and universally admired and liked could stoop to her, who had nothing but love and worship to give in return – that love was now gone and was not missed, so much greater and more satisfying was the love for her boy. And now she must lose him. Two or three silent miserable days passed by while she waited for the dreadful separation, until the thought of it became unendurable and she resolved to keep her child and sacrifice everything else. Secretly she prepared for flight, getting together the few necessary things she could carry; then, with the child in her arms, she stole out one evening and began her flight, which took her all across England at its widest part, and ended at this small coast town, the best hiding-place she could think of.

The boy was a queer little fellow, healthy but colourless, with strangely beautiful grey eyes which, on first seeing them, almost startled one with their intelligence. He was shy and almost obstinately silent, but when I talked to him on certain subjects the intense suppressed interest he felt would show itself in his face, and by and by it would burst out in speech – an impetuous torrent of words in a high shrill voice. He reminded me of a lark in a cage. Watch it in its prison when the sun shines forth – when, like the captive falcon in Dante, it is 'cheated by a gleam' – its wing-tremblings, and all its little tentative motions, how the excitement grows and grows in it, until, although shut up and flight denied it, the passion can no longer be contained and it bursts out in a torrent of shrill and guttural sounds, which, if it were free and soaring, would be its song. His passion was all for nature, and his mother out of her small earnings had managed to get quite a number of volumes together for him. These he read and re-read until he knew them by heart; and on Sundays, or any other day they could take, those two lonely ones would take a basket containing their luncheon, her work and a book or two, and set out on a long ramble along the coast to pass the day in some solitary spot among the sandhills.

With these two, the gentle woman and her quiet boy over his book, and the kitchen fire to warm and dry us after each wetting, the bad weather became quite bearable although it lasted many days. And it was amazingly bad. The wind blew with a fury from the sea; it was hard to walk against it. The people in hundreds waited in their dull apartments for a lull, and when it came they poured out like hungry sheep from the fold, or like children from a school, swarming over the green slope down to the beach, to scatter far and wide over the sands. Then, in a little while; a new menacing blackness would come up out of the sea, and by and by a fresh storm of wind would send the people scuttling back into shelter. So it went on day after day, and when night came the sound of the ever-troubled sea grew louder, so that, shut up in our little rooms in that back street, we had it in our ears, except at intervals, when the wind howled loud enough to drown its great voice, and hurled tempests of rain and hail against the roofs and windows.

To me the most amazing thing was the spectacle of the swifts. It was late for them, near the end of August; they should now have been far away on their flight to Africa; yet here they were, delaying on that desolate east coast in wind and wet, more than a hundred of them. It was strange to see so many at one spot, and I could only suppose that they had congregated previous to migration at that unsuitable place, and were being kept back by the late breeders, who had not yet been wrought up to the point of abandoning their broods. They haunted a vast ruinous old barn-like building near the front, which was probably old a century before the town was built, and about fifteen to twenty pairs had their nests under the eaves. Over this building they hung all day in a crowd, rising high to come down again at a frantic speed, and at each descent a few birds could be seen to enter the holes, while others rushed out to join the throng, and then all rose and came down again and swept round and round in a furious chase, shrieking as if mad. At all hours they drew me to that spot, and standing there, marvelling at their swaying power and the fury that possessed them, they appeared to me like tormented beings, and were like those doomed wretches in the halls of Eblis whose hearts were in a blaze of unquenchable fire, and who, every one with hands pressed to his breast, went spinning round in an everlasting agonized dance. They were tormented and crazed by the two most powerful instincts of birds pulling in opposite directions – the parental instinct and the passion of migration which called them to the south.

In such weather, especially on that naked desolate coast, exposed to the fury of the winds, one marvels at our modern craze for the sea; not merely to come and gaze upon and listen to it, to renew our youth in its salt, exhilarating waters and to lie in delicious idleness on the warm shingle or mossy cliff; but to be always, for days and weeks and even for months, at all hours, in all weathers, close to it, with its murmur, 'as of one in pain,' for ever in our ears. Undoubtedly it is an unnatural, a diseased want in us, the result of a life too confined and artificial in close dirty overcrowded cities. It is to satisfy this craving that towns have sprung up everywhere on our coasts and extended their ugly fronts for miles and leagues, with their tens of thousands of windows from which the city-sickened wretches may gaze and gaze and listen and feed their sick souls with the ocean. That is to say, during their indoor hours; at other times they walk or sit or lie as close as they can to it, following the water as it ebbs and reluctantly retiring before it when it returns. It was not so formerly, before the discovery was made that the sea could cure us. Probably our great-grandfathers didn't even know they were sick; at all events, those who had to live in the vicinity of the sea were satisfied to be a little distance from it, out of sight of its grey desolation and, if possible, out of hearing of its 'accents disconsolate.' This may be seen anywhere on our coasts; excepting the seaports and fishing settlements, the towns and villages are almost always some distance from the sea, often in a hollow or at all events screened by rising ground and woods from it. The modern seaside place has, in most cases, its old town or village not far away but quite as near as the healthy ancients wished to be.

The old village nearest to our little naked and ugly modern town was discovered at a distance of about two miles, but it might have been two hundred, so great was the change to its sheltered atmosphere. Loitering in its quiet streets among the old picturesque brick houses with tiled or thatched roofs and tall chimneys – ivy and rose and creeper-covered, with a background of old oaks and elms – I had the sensation of having come back to my own home. In that still air you could hear men and women talking fifty or a hundred yards away, the cry or laugh of a child and the clear crowing of a cock, also the smaller aerial sounds of nature, the tinkling notes of tits and other birdlings in the trees, the twitter of swallows and martins, and the 'lisp of leaves and ripple of rain.' It was sweet and restful in that home-like place, and hard to leave it to go back to the front to face the furious blasts once more. But there were compensations.

The little town, we have seen, was overcrowded with late summer visitors, all eager for the sea yet compelled to waste so much precious time shut up in apartments, and at every appearance of a slight improvement in the weather they would pour out of the houses and the green slope would be covered with a crowd of many hundreds, all hurrying down to the beach. The crowd was composed mostly of women – about three to every man, I should say – and their children; and it was one of the most interesting crowds I had ever come across on account of the large number of persons in it of a peculiarly fine type, which chance had brought together at that spot. It was the large English blonde, and there were so many individuals of this type that they gave a character to the crowd so that those of a different physique and colour appeared to be fewer than they were and were almost overlooked. They came from various places about the country, in the north and the Midlands, and appeared to be of the well-to-do classes; they, or many of them, were with their families but without their lords. They were mostly tall and large in every way, very white-skinned, with light or golden hair and large light blue eyes. A common character of these women was their quiet reposeful manner; they walked and talked and rose up and sat down and did everything, in fact, with an air of deliberation; they gazed in a slow steady way at you, and were dignified, some even majestic, and were like a herd of large beautiful white cows. The children, too, especially the girls, some almost as tall as their large mothers, though still in short frocks, were very fine. The one pastime of these was paddling, and it was a delight to see their bare feet and legs. The legs of those who had been longest on the spot – probably several weeks in some instances – were of a deep nutty brown hue suffused with pink; after these a gradation of colour, light brown tinged with buff, pinkish buff and cream, like the Gloire de Dijon rose; and so on to the delicate tender pink of the clover blossom; and, finally, the purest ivory white of the latest arrivals whose skins had not yet been caressed and coloured by sun and wind.

How beautiful are the feet of these girls by the sea who bring us glad tidings of a better time to come and the day of a nobler courage, a freer larger life when garments which have long oppressed and hindered shall have been cast away!

It was, as I have said, mere chance which had brought so many persons of a particular type together on this occasion, and I thought I might go there year after year and never see the like again. As a fact I did return when August came round and found a crowd of a different character. The type was there but did not predominate: it was no longer the herd of beautiful white and strawberry cows with golden horns and large placid eyes. Nothing in fact was the same, for when I looked for the swifts there were no more than about twenty birds instead of over a hundred, and although just on the eve of departure they were not behaving in the same excited manner.

Probably I should not have thought so much about that particular crowd in that tempestuous August, and remembered it so vividly, but for the presence of three persons in it and the strange contrast they made to the large white type I have described. These were a woman and her two little girls, aged about eight and ten respectively, but very small for their years. She was a little black haired and black-eyed woman with a pale sad dark face, on which some great grief or tragedy had left its shadow; very quiet and subdued in her manner; she would sit on a chair on the beach when the weather permitted, a book on her knees, while her two little ones played about, chasing and flying from the waves, or with the aid of their long poles vaulting from rock to rock. They were dressed in black frocks and scarlet blouses, which set off their beautiful small dark faces; their eyes sparkled like black diamonds, and their loose hair was a wonder to see, a black mist or cloud about their heads and necks composed of threads fine as gossamer, blacker than jet and shining like spun glass - hair that looked as if no comb or brush could ever tame its beautiful wildness. And in spirit they were what they seemed: such a wild, joyous, frolicsome spirit with such grace and fleetness one does not look for in human beings, but only in birds or in some small bird-like volatile mammal – a squirrel or a marmoset of the tropical forest, or the chinchilla of the desolate mountain slopes, the swiftest, wildest, loveliest, most airy and most vocal of small beasties. Occasionally, to watch their wonderful motions more closely and have speech with them, I followed when they raced over the sands or flew about over the slippery rocks, and felt like a cochin-china fowl, or muscovy duck, or dodo, trying to keep pace with a humming-bird. Their voices were well suited to their small brilliant forms; not loud, though high-pitched and singularly musical and penetrative, like the high clear notes of a skylark at a distance. They also reminded me of certain notes, which have a human quality, in some of our songsters – the swallow, redstart, pied wagtail, whinchat, and two or three others. Such pure and beautiful sounds are sometimes heard in human voices, chiefly in children, when they are talking and laughing in joyous excitement. But for any sort of conversation they were too volatile; before I could get a dozen words from them they would be off again, flying and flitting along the margin, like sandpipers, and beating the clear-voiced sandpiper at his own aerial graceful game.

By and by I was favoured with a fine exhibition of the spirit animating these two little things. The weather had made it possible for the crowd of visitors to go down and scatter itself over the beach, when the usual black cloud sprang up and soon burst on us in a furious tempest of wind and rain, sending the people flying back to the shelter of a large structure erected for such purposes against the cliff. It was a vast barn-like place, open to the front, the roof supported by wooden columns, and here in a few minutes some three or four hundred persons were gathered, mostly women and their girls, white and blue-eyed, with long wet golden hair hanging down their backs. Finding a vacant place on the bench, I sat down next to a large motherly-looking woman with a robust or dumpy blue-eyed girl about four or five years old on her lap. Most of the people were standing about in groups waiting for the storm to blow over, and presently I noticed my two wild-haired dark little girls moving about in the crowd. It was impossible not to see them, for they could not keep still a moment. They were here, there, and everywhere, playing hide-and-seek and skipping and racing wherever they could find an opening, and by and by, taking hold of each other, they started dancing. It was a pretty spectacle, but most interesting to see was the effect produced on the other children, the hundred girls, big and little, the little ones especially, who had been standing there tired and impatient to get out to the sea, and who were now becoming more and more excited as they gazed, until, like children when listening to lively music, they began moving feet and hands and soon their whole bodies in time to the swift movements of the little dancers. At last, plucking up courage, first one, then another, joined them, and were caught as they came and whirled round and round in a manner quite new to them and which they appeared to find very delightful. By and by I observed that the little rosy-faced dumpy girl on my neighbour's knees was taking the infection; she was staring, her blue eyes opened to their widest in wonder and delight. Then suddenly she began pleading, 'Oh, mummy, do let me go to the little girls – oh, do let me!' And her mother said 'No,' because she was so little, and could never fly round like that, and so would fall and hurt herself and cry. But she pleaded still, and was ready to cry if refused, until the good anxious mother was compelled to release her; and down she slipped, and after standing still with her little arms and closed hands held up as if to collect herself before plunging into the new tremendous adventure, she rushed out towards the dancers. One of them saw her coming, and instantly quitting the child she was waltzing with flew to meet her, and catching her round the middle began spinning her about as if the solid little thing weighed no more than a feather. But it proved too much for her; very soon she came down and broke into a loud cry, which brought her mother instantly to her, and she was picked up and taken back to the seat and held to the broad bosom and soothed with caresses and tender words until the sobs began to subside. Then, even before the tears were dry, her eyes were once more gazing at the tireless little dancers, taking on child after child as they came timidly forward to have a share in the fun, and once more she began to plead with her 'mummy,' and would not be denied, for she was a most determined little Saxon, until getting her way she rushed out for a second trial. Again the little dancer saw her coming and flew to her like a bird to its mate, and clasping her laughed her merry musical little laugh. It was her 'sudden glory,' an expression of pure delight in her power to infuse her own fire and boundless gaiety of soul into all these little blue-eyed rosy phlegmatic lumps of humanity.

What was it in these human mites, these fantastic Brownies, which, in that crowd of Rowenas and their children, made them seem like beings not only of another race, but of another species? How came they alone to be distinguished among so many by that irresponsible gaiety, as of the most volatile of wild creatures, that quickness of sense and mind and sympathy, that variety and grace and swiftness – all these brilliant exotic qualities harmoniously housed in their small beautiful elastic and vigorous frames? It was their genius, their character – something derived from their race. But what race? Looking at their mother watching her little ones at their frolics with dark shining eyes – the small oval-faced brown-skinned woman with blackest hair – I could but say that she was an Iberian, pure and simple, and that her children were like her. In Southern Europe that type abounds; it is also to be met with throughout Britain, perhaps most common in the southern counties, and it is not uncommon in East Anglia. Indeed, I think it is in Norfolk where we may best see the two most marked sub-types in which it is divided – the two extremes. The small stature, narrow head, dark skin, black hair and eyes are common to both, and in both these physical characters are correlated with certain mental traits, as, for instance, a peculiar vivacity and warmth of disposition; but they are high and low. In the latter sub-division the skin is coarse in texture, brown or old parchment in colour, with little red in it; the black hair is also coarse, the forehead small, the nose projecting, and the facial angle indicative of a more primitive race. One might imagine that these people had been interred, along with specimens of rude pottery and bone and flint implements, a long time back, about the beginning of the Bronze Age perhaps, and had now come out of their graves and put on modern clothes. At all events I don't think a resident in Norfolk would have much difficulty in picking out the portraits of some of his fellow-villagers in Mr. Reed's *Prehistoric Peeps*.

The mother and her little ones were of the higher sub-type: they had delicate skins, beautiful faces, clear musical voices. They were Iberians in blood, but improved; purified and refined as by fire; gentleized and spiritualized, and to the lower types down to the aboriginals, as is the bright consummate flower to leaf and stem and root.

Often and often we are teased and tantalized and mocked by that old question:

> Oh! so old –
> Thousands of years, thousands of years,
> If all were told –

of black and blue eyes; blue versus black and black versus blue, to put it both ways. And by black we mean black with orange-brown lights in it – the eye called tortoise-shell; and velvety browns with other browns, also hazels. Blue includes all blues, from ultramarine, or violet, to the palest blue of a pale sky; and all greys down to the grey that is almost white. Our preference for this or that colour is supposed to depend on nothing but individual taste, or fancy, and association. I believe it is something more, but I do find that we are very apt to be swayed this way and that by the colour of the eyes of the people we meet in life, according as they (the people) attract or repel us. The eyes of the two little girls were black as polished black diamonds until looked at closely, when they appeared a beautiful deep brown on which the black pupils were seen distinctly; they were so lovely that I, predisposed to prefer dark to light, felt that this question was now definitely settled for me – that black was best. That irresistible charm, the flame-like spirit which raised these two so much above the others – how could it go with anything but the darkest eyes!

But no sooner was the question thus settled definitely and for all time, to my very great satisfaction, than it was unsettled again. I do not know how this came about; it may have been the sight of some small child's blue eyes looking up at me, like the arch blue eyes of a kitten, full of wonder at the world and everything in it;

> 'Where did you get those eyes so blue?'
> 'Out of the sky as I came through';

or it may have been the sight of a harebell; and perhaps it came from nothing but the 'waste shining of the sky.' At all events, there they were, remembered again, looking at me from the past, blue eyes that were beautiful and dear to me, whose blue colour was associated with every sweetness and charm in child and woman and with all that is best and highest in human souls; and I could not and had no wish to resist their appeal.

Then came a new experience of the eye that is blue – a meeting with one who almost seemed to be less flesh than spirit. A middle-aged lady, frail, very frail; exceedingly pale from long ill-health, prematurely white-haired, with beautiful grey eyes, gentle but wonderfully bright. Altogether she was like a being compounded as to her grosser part of foam and mist and gossamer and thistledown, and was swayed by every breath of air, and who, should she venture abroad in rough weather, would be lifted and blown away by the gale and scattered like mist over the earth. Yet she, so frail, so timid, was the one member of the community who had set herself to do the work of a giant – that of championing all ill-used and suffering creatures, wild or tame, holding a protecting shield over them against the innate brutality of the people. She had been abused and mocked and jeered at by many, while others had regarded her action with an amused smile or else with a cold indifference. But eventually some, for very shame, had been drawn to her side, and a change in the feeling of the people had resulted; domestic animals were treated better, and it was no longer universally believed that all wild animals, especially those with wings, existed only that men might amuse themselves by killing and wounding and trapping and caging and persecuting them in various other ways.

The sight of that burning and shining spirit in its frail tenement – for did I not actually see her spirit and the very soul of her in those eyes? – was the last of the unforgotten experiences I had at that place which had startled and repelled me with its ugliness.

But, no, there was one more, marvellous as any – the experience of a day of days, one of those rare days when nature appears to us spiritualized and is no longer nature, when that which had transfigured this visible world is in us too, and it becomes possible to believe – it is almost a conviction – that the burning and shining spirit seen and recognized in one among a thousand we have known is in all of us and in all things. In such moments it is possible to go beyond even the most advanced of the modern physicists who hold that force alone exists, that matter is but a disguise, a shadow and delusion; for we may add that force itself – that which we call force or energy – is but a semblance and shadow of the universal soul.

The change in the weather was not sudden; the furious winds dropped gradually; the clouds floated higher in the heavens, and were of a lighter grey; there were wider breaks in them, showing the lucid blue beyond; and the sea grew quieter. It had raved and roared too long, beating against the iron walls that held it back, and was now spent and fallen into an uneasy sleep, but still moved uneasily and moaned a little. Then all at once summer returned, coming like a thief in the night, for when it was morning the sun rose in splendour and power in a sky without a cloud on its vast azure expanse, on a calm sea with no motion but that scarcely perceptible rise and fall as of one that sleeps. As the sun rose higher the air grew warmer until it was full summer heat, but although a 'visible heat,' it was never oppressive; for all that day we were abroad, and as the tide ebbed a new country that was neither earth nor sea was disclosed, an infinite expanse of pale yellow sand stretching away on either side, and further and further out until it mingled and melted into the sparkling water and faintly seen line of foam on the horizon. And over all – the distant sea, the ridge of low dunes marking where the earth ended and the flat, yellow expanse between – there brooded a soft bluish silvery haze. A haze that blotted nothing out, but blended and interfused them all until earth and air and sea and sands were scarcely distinguishable. The effect, delicate, mysterious, unearthly, cannot be described.

> Ethereal gauze...
> Visible heat, air-water, and dry sea,
> Last conquest of the eye...
> Sun-dust,
> Aerial surf upon the shores of earth,
> Ethereal estuary, frith of light....
> Bird of the sun, transparent-winged.

Do we not see that words fail as pigments do – that the effect is too coarse, since in describing it we put it before the mental eye as something distinctly visible, a thing of itself and separate. But it is not so in nature; the effect is of something almost invisible and is yet a part of all and makes all things – sky and sea and land – as unsubstantial as itself. Even living, moving things had that aspect. Far out on the lowest further strip of sand, which appeared to be on a level with the sea, gulls were seen standing in twos and threes and small groups and in rows; but they did not look like gulls – familiar birds, gull-shaped with grey and white plumage. They appeared twice as big as gulls, and were of a dazzling whiteness and of no definite shape: though standing still they had motion, an effect of the quivering dancing air, the 'visible heat'; at rest, they were seen now as separate objects; then as one with the silver sparkle on the sea; and when they rose and floated away they were no longer shining and white, but like pale shadows of winged forms faintly visible in the haze.

They were not birds but spirits – beings that lived in or were passing through the world and now, like the heat, made visible; and I, standing far out on the sparkling sands, with the sparkling sea on one side and the line of dunes, indistinctly seen as land, on the other, was one of them; and if any person had looked at me from a distance he would have seen me as a formless shining white being standing by the sea, and then perhaps as a winged shadow floating in the haze. It was only necessary to put out one's arms to float. That was the effect on my mind: this natural world was changed to a supernatural, and there was no more matter nor force in sea or land nor in the heavens above, but only spirit.

CHAPTER SIX

By Swallowfield

One of the most attractive bits of green and wooded country near London I know lies between Reading and Basingstoke and includes Aldermaston with its immemorial oaks in Berkshire and Silchester with Pamber Forest in Hampshire. It has long been one of my favourite haunts, summer and winter, and it is perhaps the only wooded place in England where I have a home feeling as strong as that which I experience in certain places among the South Wiltshire downs and in the absolutely flat country on the Severn, in Somerset, and the flat country in Cambridgeshire and East Anglia, especially at Lynn and about Ely.

I am now going back to my first visit to this green retreat; it was in the course of one of those Easter walks I have spoken of, and the way was through Reading and by Three Mile Cross and Swallowfield. On this occasion I conceived a dislike to Reading which I have never quite got over, for it seemed an unconscionably big place for two slow pedestrians to leave behind. Worse still, when we did leave it we found that Reading would not leave us. It was like a stupendous octopus in red brick which threw out red tentacles, miles and miles long in various directions – little rows and single and double cottages and villas, all in red, red brick and its weary accompaniment, the everlasting hard slate roof. These square red brick boxes with sloping slate tops are built as close as possible to the public road, so that the passer-by looking in at the windows may see the whole interior – wall-papers, pictures, furniture, and oftentimes the dull expressionless face of the woman of the house, staring back at you out of her shallow blue eyes. The weather too was against us; a grey hard sky, like the slate roofs, and a cold strong east wind to make the road dusty all day long.

Arrived at Three Mile Cross, it was no surprise to find it no longer recognizable as the hamlet described in *Our Village*, but it was saddening to look at the cottage in which Mary Russell Mitford lived and was on the whole very happy with her flowers and work for thirty years of her life, in its present degraded state. It has a sign now and calls itself the 'Mitford Arms' and a 'Temperance Hotel,' and we were told that you could get tea and bread and butter there but nothing else. The cottage has been much altered since Miss Mitford's time, and the open space once occupied by the beloved garden is now filled with buildings, including a corrugated-iron dissenting chapel.

From Three Mile Cross we walked on to Swallowfield, still by those never-ending roadside red-brick cottages and villas, for we were not yet properly out of the hated biscuit metropolis. It was a big village with the houses scattered far and wide over several square miles of country, but just where the church stands it is shady and pleasant. The pretty churchyard too is very deeply shaded and occupies a small hill with the Loddon flowing partly round it, then taking its swift way through the village. Miss Mitford's monument is a plain, almost an ugly, granite cross, standing close to the wall, shaded by yew, elm, and beech trees, and one is grateful to think that if she never had her reward when living she has found at any rate a very peaceful resting-place.

The sexton was there and told us that he was but ten years old when Miss Mitford died, but that he remembered her well and she was a very pleasant little woman. Others in the place who remembered her said the same – that she was very pleasant and sweet. We know that she was sweet and charming, but unfortunately the portraits we have of her do not give that impression. They represent her as a fat common-place looking person, a little vulgar perhaps. I fancy the artists were bunglers. I possess a copy of a very small pencil sketch made of her face by a dear old lady friend of mine, now dead, about the year 1851 or 2. My friend had a gift for portraiture in a peculiar way. When she saw a face that greatly interested her, in a drawing-room, on a platform, in the street, anywhere, it remained very vividly in her mind and on going home she would sketch it, and some of these sketches of well-known persons are wonderfully good. She was staying in the country with a friend who drove with her to Swallowfield to call on Miss Mitford, and on her return to her friend's house she made the little sketch, and in this tiny portrait I can see the refinement, the sweetness, the animation and charm which she undoubtedly possessed.

But let me now venture to step a little outside of my own province, my small plot – a poor pedestrian's unimportant impressions of places and faces; all these p's come by accident; and this I put in parenthetically just because an editor solemnly told me a while ago that he couldn't abide and wouldn't have alliteration's artful aid in his periodical. Let us leave the subject of what Miss Mitford was to those of her day who knew her; a thousand lovely personalities pass away every year and in a little while are no more remembered than the bright-plumaged bird that falls in the tropical forest, or the vanished orchid bloom of which some one has said that the angels in heaven can look on no more beautiful thing. Leaving all that, let us ask what remains to us of another generation of all she was and did?

She was a prolific writer, both prose and verse, and, as we know, had an extraordinary vogue in her own time. Anything that came from her pen had immediate success; indeed, so highly was she regarded that nothing she chose to write, however poor, could fail. And she certainly did write a good deal of poor stuff: it was all in a sense poor, but books and books, poor soul, she had to write. It was in a sense poor because it was mostly ambitious stuff, and, as the proverb says, 'You cannot fly like an eagle with the wings of a wren.' She was driven to fly, and gave her little wings too much to do, and her flights were apt to be mere little weak flutterings over the surface of the ground. A wren, and she had not a cuckoo but a devouring cormorant to sustain – that dear, beautiful father of hers, who was more to her than any reprobate son to his devoted mother, and who day after day, year after year, gobbled up her earnings, and then would hungrily go on squawking for more until he stumbled into the grave. Alas! he was too long in dying; she was worn out by then, the little heart beating not so fast, and the bright little brain growing dim and very tired.

Now all the ambitious stuff she wrote to keep the cormorant and, incidentally, to immortalize herself, has fallen deservedly into oblivion. But we – some of us – do not forget and never want to forget Mary Russell Mitford. Her letters remain – the little friendly letters which came from her pen like balls of silvery down from a sun-ripened plant, and were wafted far and wide over the land to those she loved. There is a wonderful charm in them; they are so spontaneous, so natural, so perfectly reflect her humour and vivacity, her overflowing sweetness, her beautiful spirit. And one book too remains – the series of sketches about the poor little hamlet, in which she lived so long and laboured so hard to support herself and her parents, the turtledove mated with a cormorant. Driven to produce work and hard up for a subject, in a happy moment she took up this humble one lying at her own door and allowed herself to write naturally even as in her most intimate letters. This is the reason of the vitality of *Our Village*; it was simple, natural, and reflected the author herself, her tender human heart, her impulsive nature, her bright playful humorous spirit. There is no thought, no mind stuff in it, and it is a classic! It is about the country, and she has so little observation that it might have been written in a town, out of a book, away from nature's sights and sounds. Her rustic characters are not comparable to those of a score or perhaps two or three score of other writers who treat of such subjects. The dialogue, when she makes them talk, is unnatural, and her invention so poor that when she puts in a little romance of her own making one regrets it. And so one might go on picking it all to pieces like a dandelion blossom. Nevertheless it endures, outliving scores of in a way better books on the same themes, because her own delightful personality manifests itself and shines in all these little pictures. This short passage describing how she took Lizzie, the little village child she loved, to gather cowslips in the meadows, will serve as an illustration.

They who know these feelings (and who is so happy as not to have known some of them) will understand why Alfieri became powerless, and Froissart dull; and why even needlework, the most effective sedative, that grand soother and composer of women's distress, fails to comfort me today. I will go out into the air this cool, pleasant afternoon, and try what that will do … . I will go to the meadows, the beautiful meadows and I will have my materials of happiness, Lizzie and May, and a basket for flowers, and we will make a cowslip ball. 'Did you ever see a cowslip ball, Lizzie?' 'No.' 'Come away then; make haste! run, Lizzie!'

And on we go, fast, fast! down the road, across the lea, past the workhouse, along by the great pond, till we slide into the deep narrow lane, whose hedges seem to meet over the water, and win our way to the little farmhouse at the end. 'Through the farmyard, Lizzie; over the gate; never mind the cows; they are quiet enough.' 'I don't mind 'em,' said Miss Lizzie, boldly and truly, and with a proud affronted air, displeased at being thought to mind anything, and showing by her attitude and manner some design of proving her courage by an attack on the largest of the herd, in the shape of a pull by the tail. 'I don't mind 'em.' 'I know you don't, Lizzie; but let them alone and don't chase the turkey-cock. Come to me, my dear!' and, for a wonder, Lizzie came.

In the meantime my other pet, Mayflower, had also gotten into a scrape. She had driven about a huge unwieldy sow, till the animal's grunting had disturbed the repose of a still more enormous Newfoundland dog, the guardian of the yard.

The beautiful white greyhound's mocking treatment of the surly dog on the chain then follows, and other pretty scenes and adventures, until after some mishaps and much trouble the cowslip ball is at length completed.

> What a concentration of fragrance and beauty it was! Golden and sweet to satiety! rich to sight, and touch, and smell! Lizzie was enchanted, and ran off with her prize, hiding amongst the trees in the very coyness of ecstasy, as if any human eye, even mine, would be a restraint on her innocent raptures.

Here the very woman is revealed to us, her tender and lively disposition, her impulsiveness and childlike love of fun and delight in everything on earth. We see in such a passage what her merit really is, the reason of our liking or 'partiality' for her. Her pleasure in everything makes everything interesting, and in displaying her feeling without art or disguise she succeeds in giving what we may call a literary expression to personal charm – that quality which is almost untranslatable into written words. Many women possess it; it is in them and issues from them, and is like an essential oil in a flower, but too volatile to be captured and made use of. Furthermore, women when they write are as a rule even more conventional than men, more artificial and out of and away from themselves.

I do not know that any literary person will agree with me; I have gone aside to write about Miss Mitford mainly for my own satisfaction. Frequently when I have wanted to waste half an hour pleasantly with a book I have found myself picking up *Our Village* from among many others, some waiting for a first perusal, and I wanted to know why this was so – to find out, if not to invent, some reason for my liking which would not make me ashamed.

At Swallowfield we failed to find a place to stay at; there was no such place; and of the inns, named, I think, the 'Crown,' 'Cricketers,' 'Bird-in-the-Hand,' and 'George and Dragon,' only one, was said to provide accommodation for travellers as the law orders, but on going to the house we were informed that the landlord or his wife was just dead, or dangerously ill, I forget which, and they could take no one in. Accordingly, we had to trudge back to Three Mile Cross and the old ramshackle, well-nigh ruinous inn there. It was a wretched place, smelling of mould and dry-rot; however, it was not so bad after a fire had been lighted in the grate, but first the young girl who waited on us brought in a bundle of newspapers, which she proceeded to thrust up the chimney-flue and kindle, 'to warm the flue and make the fire burn,' she explained.

On the following day, the weather being milder, we rambled on through woods and lanes, visiting several villages, and arrived in the afternoon at Silchester, where we had resolved to put up for the night. By a happy chance we found a pleasant cottage on the common to stay at and pleasant people in it, so that we were glad to sit down for a week there, to loiter about the furzy waste, or prowl in the forest and haunt the old walls; but it was pleasant even indoors with that wide prospect before the window, the wooded country stretching many miles away to the hills of Kingsclere, blue in the distance and crowned with their beechen rings and groves. Of Roman Calleva itself and the thoughts I had there I will write in the following chapter; here I will only relate how on Easter Sunday, two days after arriving, we went to morning service in the old church standing on a mound inside the walls, a mile from the village and common.

It came to pass that during the service the sun began to shine very brightly after several days of cloud and misty windy wet weather, and that brilliance and the warmth in it served to bring a butterfly out of hiding; then another; then a third; red admirals all; and they were seen through all the prayers, and psalms, and hymns, and lessons, and the sermon preached by the white-haired rector, fluttering against the translucent glass, wanting to be out in that splendour and renew their life after so long a period of suspension. But the glass was between them and their world of blue heavens and woods and meadow flowers; then I thought that after the service I would make an attempt to get them out; but soon reflected that to release them it would be necessary to capture them first, and that that could not be done without a ladder and butterfly net. Among the women (ladies) on either side of and before me there were no fewer than five wearing aigrettes of egret and bird-of-paradise plumes in their hats or bonnets, and these five all remained to take part in that ceremony of eating bread and drinking wine in remembrance of an event supposed to be of importance to their souls, here and hereafter. It saddened me to leave my poor red admirals in their prison, beating their red wings against the coloured glass – to leave them too in such company, where the aigrette wearers were worshipping a little god of their own little imaginations, who did not create and does not regard the swallow and dove and white egret and bird-of-paradise, and who was therefore not my god and whose will as they understood it was nothing to me.

It was a consolation when I went out, still thinking of the butterflies in their prison, and stood by the old ruined walls grown over with ivy and crowned with oak and holly trees, to think that in another two thousand years there will be no archaeologist and no soul in Silchester, or anywhere else in Britain, or in the world, who would take the trouble to dig up the remains of aigrette-wearers and their works, and who would care what had become of their pitiful little souls – their immortal part.

CHAPTER SEVEN

Roman Calleva

An afternoon in the late November of 1903. Frost, gales, and abundant rains have more than half stripped the oaks of their yellow leaves. But the rain is over now, the sky once more a pure lucid blue above me – all around me, in fact, since I am standing high on the top of the ancient stupendous earthwork, grown over with oak wood and underwood of holly and thorn and hazel with tangle of ivy and bramble and briar. It is marvellously still; no sound from the village reaches me; I only hear the faint rustle of the dead leaves as they fall, and the robin, for one has spied me here and has come to keep me company. At intervals he spurts out his brilliant little fountain of sound; and that sudden bright melody and the bright colour of the sunlit translucent leaves seem like one thing. Nature is still, and I am still, standing concealed among trees, or moving cautiously through the dead russet bracken. Not that I am expecting to get a glimpse of the badger who has his hermitage in this solitary place, but I am on forbidden ground, in the heart of a sacred pheasant preserve, where one must do one's prowling warily. Hard by, almost within a stone's-throw of the wood-grown earthwork on which I stand, are the ruinous walls of Roman Calleva – the Silchester which the antiquarians have been occupied in uncovering these dozen years or longer. The stone walls, too, like the more ancient earthwork, are overgrown with trees and brambles and ivy. The trees have grown upon the wall, sending roots deep down between the stones, through the crumbling cement; and so fast are they anchored that never a tree falls but it brings down huge masses of masonry with it. This slow levelling process has been going on for centuries, and it was doubtless in this way that the buildings within the walls were pulled down long ages ago. Then the action of the earthworms began, and floors and foundations, with fallen stones and tiles, were gradually buried in the soil, and what was once a city was a dense thicket of oak and holly and thorn. Finally the wood was cleared, and the city was a walled wheat field – so far as we know, the ground has been cultivated since the days of King John. But the entire history of this green walled space before me – less than twenty centuries in duration – does not seem so very long compared with that of the huge earthen wall I am standing on, which dates back to prehistoric times.

Standing here, knee-deep in the dead ruddy bracken, in the 'coloured shade' of the oaks, idly watching the leaves fall fluttering to the ground, thinking in an aimless way of the remains of the two ancient cities before me, the British and the Roman, and of their comparative antiquity, I am struck with the thought that the sweet sensations produced in me by the scene differ in character from the feeling I have had in other solitary places. The peculiar sense of satisfaction, of restfulness, of peace, experienced here is very perfect; but in the wilderness, where man has never been, or has at all events left no trace of his former presence, there is ever a mysterious sense of loneliness, of desolation, underlying our pleasure in nature. Here it seems good to know, or to imagine, that the men I occasionally meet in my solitary rambles, and those I see in the scattered rustic village hard by, are of the same race, and possibly the descendants, of the people who occupied this spot in the remote past – Iberian and Celt, and Roman and Saxon and Dane. If that hard-featured and sour-visaged old gamekeeper, with the cold blue unfriendly eyes, should come upon me here in my hiding-place, and scowl as he is accustomed to do, standing silent before me, gun in hand, to hear my excuses for trespassing in his preserves, I should say (mentally): This man is distinctly English, and his far-off progenitors, somewhere about sixteen hundred years ago, probably assisted at the massacre of the inhabitants of the pleasant little city at my feet. By and by, leaving the ruins, I may meet with other villagers of different features and different colour in hair, skin, and eyes, and of a pleasanter expression; and in them I may see the remote descendants of other older races of men, some who were lords here before the Romans came, and of others before them, even back to Neolithic times.

This, I take it, is a satisfaction, a sweetness and peace to the soul in nature, because it carries with it a sense of the continuity of the human race, its undying vigour, its everlastingness. After all the tempests that have overcome it, through all mutations in such immense stretches of time, how stable it is!

I recall the time when I lived on a vast vacant level green plain, an earth which to the eye, and to the mind which sees with the eye, appeared illimitable, like the ocean; where the house I was born in was the oldest in the district – a century old, it was said; where the people were the children's children of emigrants from Europe who had conquered and colonized the country, and had enjoyed but half a century of national life. But the people who had possessed the land before these emigrants – what of them? They were but a memory, a tradition, a story told in books and hardly more to us than a fable; perhaps they had dwelt there for long centuries, or for thousands of years; perhaps they had come, a wandering horde, to pass quickly away like a flight of migrating locusts; for no memorial existed, no work of their hands, not the faintest trace of their occupancy.

Walking one day at the side of a ditch, which had been newly cut through a meadow at the end of our plantation, I caught sight of a small black object protruding from the side of the cutting, which turned out to be a fragment of Indian pottery made of coarse clay, very black, and rudely ornamented on one side. On searching further a few more pieces were found. I took them home and preserved them carefully, experiencing a novel and keen sense of pleasure in their possession; for though worthless, they were man's handiwork, the only real evidence I had come upon of that vanished people who had been before us; and it was as if those bits of baked clay, with a pattern incised on them by a man's finger-nail, had in them some magical property which enabled me to realize the past, and to see that vacant plain repeopled with long dead and forgotten men.

Doubtless we all possess the feeling in some degree – the sense of loneliness and desolation and dismay at the thought of an uninhabited world, and of long periods when man was not. Is it not the absence of human life or remains rather than the illimitable wastes of thick-ribbed ice and snow which daunts us at the thought of Arctic and Antarctic regions? Again, in the story of the earth, as told by geology, do we not also experience the same sense of dismay, and the soul shrinking back on itself, when we come in imagination to those deserts desolate in time when the continuity of the race was broken and the world dispeopled? The doctrine of evolution has made us tolerant of the thought of human animals – our progenitors as we must believe – who were of brutish aspect, and whose period on this planet was so long that, compared with it, the historic and prehistoric periods are but as the life of an individual. A quarter of a million years has perhaps elapsed since the beginning of that cold period which, at all events in this part of the earth, killed Palaeolithic man; yet how small a part of his racial life even that time would seem if, as some believe, his remains may be traced as far back as the Eocene! But after this rude man of the Quaternary and Tertiary epochs had passed away there is a void, a period which to the imagination seems measureless, when sun and moon and stars looked on a waste and mindless world. When man once more reappears he seems to have been re-created on somewhat different lines.

It is this break in the history of the human race which amazes and daunts us, which 'shadows forth the heartless voids and immensities of the universe, *and thus stabs us from behind with the thought of annihilation.*'

Here, in these words of Herman Melville, we are let all at once into the true meaning of those disquieting and seemingly indefinable emotions so often experienced, even by the most ardent lovers of nature and of solitude, in uninhabited deserts, on great mountains, and on the sea. We find here the origin of that horror of mountains which was so common until recent times. A friend once confessed to me that he was always profoundly unhappy at sea during long voyages, and the reason was that his sustaining belief in a superintending Power and in immortality left him when he was on that waste of waters, which have no human associations. The feeling, so intense in his case, is known to most if not all of us; but we feel it faintly as a disquieting element in nature of which we may be but vaguely conscious.

Most travelled Englishmen who have seen much of the world and resided for long or short periods in many widely separated countries would probably agree that there is a vast difference in the feeling of strangeness, or want of harmony with our surroundings, experienced in old and in new countries. It is a compound feeling and some of its elements are the same in both cases; but in one there is a disquieting element which the other is without. Thus, in Southern Europe, Egypt, Syria, and in many countries of Asia, and some portions of Africa, the wanderer from home might experience dissatisfaction and be ill at ease and wish for old familiar sights and sounds; but in a colony like Tasmania, and in any new country where there were no remains of antiquity, no links with the past, the feeling would be very much more poignant, and in some scenes and moods would be like that sense of desolation which assails us at the thought of the heartless voids and immensities of the universe.

He recognizes that he is in a world on which we have but recently entered, and in which our position is not yet assured.

Here, standing on this mound, as on other occasions past count-
ing, I recognize and appreciate the enormous difference which human
associations make in the effect produced on us by visible nature. In
this silent solitary place, with the walled field which was once Calleva
Atrebatum at my feet, I yet have a sense of satisfaction, of security,
never felt in a land that had no historic past. The knowledge that my
individual life is but a span, a breath; that in a little while I too must
wither and mingle like one of those fallen yellow leaves with the mould,
does not grieve me. I know it and yet disbelieve it; for am I not here
alive, where men have inhabited for thousands of years, feeling what I
now feel – their oneness with everlasting nature and the undying human
family? The very soil and wet carpet of moss on which their feet were
set, the standing trees and leaves, green or yellow, the rain-drops, the air
they breathed, the sunshine in their eyes and hearts, was part of them,
not a garment, but of their very substance and spirit. Feeling this, death
becomes an illusion; and the illusion that the continuous life of the
species (its immortality) and the individual life are one and the same is
the reality and truth. An illusion, but, as Mill says, deprive us of our illu-
sions and life would be intolerable. Happily we are not easily deprived
of them, since they are of the nature of instincts and ineradicable. And
this very one which our reason can prove to be the most childish, the
absurdest of all, is yet the greatest, the most fruitful of good for the race.
To those who have discarded supernatural religion, it may be a religion,
or at all events the foundation to build one on. For there is no comfort
to the healthy natural man in being told that the good he does will not
be interred with his bones, since he does not wish to think, and in fact
refuses to think, that his bones will ever be interred. Joy in the 'choir
invisible' is to him a mere poetic fancy, or at best a rarefied transcenden-
talism, which fails to sustain him. If altruism, or the religion of humanity, is a living vigorous plant, and as some believe flourishes more with
the progress of the centuries, it must, like other 'soul-growths,' have a
deeper, tougher, woodier root in our soil.

CHAPTER EIGHT

A Cold Day at Silchester

It is little to a man's profit to go far afield if his chief pleasure be in wild life, his main object to get nearer to the creatures, to grow day by day more intimate with them, and to see each day some new thing. Yet the distance has the same fascination for him as for another – the call is as sweet and persistent in his ears. If he is on a green level country with blue hills on the horizon, then, especially in the early morning, is the call sweetest, most irresistible. Come away – come away: this blue world has better things than any in that green, too familiar place. The startling scream of the jay – you have heard it a thousand times. It is pretty to watch the squirrel in his chestnut-red coat among the oaks in their fresh green foliage, full of fun as a bright child, eating his apple like a child, only it is an oak-apple, shining white or white and rosy-red, in his little paws; but you have seen it so many times – come away!

It was not this voice alone which made me forsake the green oaks of Silchester and Pamber Forest, to ramble for a season hither and thither in Wiltshire, Dorset, and Somerset; there was something for me to do in those places, but the call made me glad to go. And long weeks – months – went by in my wanderings, mostly in open downland country, too often under gloomy skies, chilled by cold winds and wetted by cold rains. Then, having accomplished my purpose and discovered incidentally that the call had mocked me again, as on so many previous occasions, I returned once more to the old familiar green place.

Crossing the common, I found that where it had been dry in spring one might now sink to his knees in the bog; also that the snipe which had vanished for a season were back at the old spot where they used to breed. It was a bitter day near the end of an unpleasant summer, with the wind back in the old hateful north-east quarter; but the sun shone, the sky was blue, and the flying clouds were of a dazzling whiteness. Shivering, I remembered the south wall, and went there, since to escape from the wind and bask like some half-frozen serpent or lizard in the heat was the highest good one could look for in such weather. To see anything new in wild life was not to be hoped for.

That old grey, crumbling wall of ancient Calleva, crowned with big oak and ash and thorn and holly, and draped with green bramble and trailing ivy and creepers – how good a shelter it is on a cold, rough day! Moving softly, so as not to disturb any creature, I yet disturbed a ring snake lying close to the wall, into which it quickly vanished; and then from their old place among the stones a pair of blue stock-doves rushed out with clatter of wings. The same blue doves which I had known for three years at that spot! A few more steps and I came upon as pretty a little scene in bird life as one could wish for: twenty to twenty-five small birds of different species – tits, wrens, dunnocks, thrushes, blackbirds, chaffinches, yellowhammers – were congregated on the lower outside twigs of a bramble bush and on the bare ground beside it close to the foot of the wall. The sun shone full on that spot, and they had met for warmth and for company. The tits and wrens were moving quietly about in the bush; others were sitting idly or preening their feathers on the twigs or the ground. Most of them were making some kind of small sound – little exclamatory chirps, and a variety of chirrupings, producing the effect of a pleasant conversation going on among them. This was suddenly suspended on my appearance, but the alarm was soon over, and, seeing me seated on a fallen stone and motionless, they took no further notice of me. Two blackbirds were there, sitting a little way apart on the bare ground; these were silent, the raggedest, rustiest-looking members of that little company; for they were moulting, and their drooping wings and tails had many unsightly gaps in them where the old feathers had dropped out before the new ones had grown. They were suffering from that annual sickness with temporary loss of their brightest faculties which all birds experience in some degree; the unseasonable rains and cold winds had been bad for them, and now they were having their sun-bath, their best medicine and cure.

By and by a pert-looking, bright-feathered, dapper cock chaffinch dropped down from the bush, and, advancing to one of the two, the rustiest and most forlorn-looking, started running round and round him as if to make a close inspection of his figure, then began to tease him. At first I thought it was all in fun – merely animal spirit which in birds often discharges itself in this way in little pretended attacks and fights. But the blackbird had no play and no fight in him, no heart to defend himself; all he did was to try to avoid the strokes aimed at him, and he could not always escape them. His spiritlessness served to inspire the chaffinch with greater boldness, and then it appeared that the gay little creature was really and truly incensed, possibly because the rusty, draggled, and listless appearance of the larger bird was offensive to him. Anyhow, the persecutions continued, increasing in fury until they could not be borne, and the blackbird tried to escape by hiding in the bramble. But he was not permitted to rest there; out he was soon driven and away into another bush, and again into still another further away, and finally he was hunted over the sheltering wall into the bleak wind on the other side. Then the persecutor came back and settled himself on his old perch on the bramble, well satisfied at his victory over a bird so much bigger than himself. All was again peace and harmony in the little social gathering, and the pleasant talkee-talkee went on as before. About five minutes passed, then the hunted blackbird returned, and, going to the identical spot from which he had been driven, composed himself to rest; only now he sat facing his lively little enemy.

I was astonished to see him back; so, apparently, was the chaffinch. He started, craned his neck, and regarded his adversary first with one eye then with the other. 'What, rags and tatters, back again so soon!' I seem to hear him say. 'You miserable travesty of a bird, scarcely fit for a weasel to dine on! Your presence is an insult to us, but I'll soon settle you. You'll feel the cold on the other side of the wall when I've knocked off a few more of your rusty rags.'

Down from his perch he came, but no sooner had he touched his feet to the ground than the blackbird went straight at him with extraordinary fury. The chaffinch, taken by surprise, was buffeted and knocked over, then, recovering himself, fled in consternation, hotly pursued by the sick one. Into the bush they went, but in a moment they were out again, darting this way and that, now high up in the trees, now down to the ground, the blackbird always close behind; and no little bird flying from a hawk could have exhibited a greater terror than that pert chaffinch – that vivacious and most pugnacious little cock bantam. At last they went quite away, and were lost to sight. By and by the blackbird returned alone, and, going once more to his place near the second bird, he settled down comfortably to finish his sunbath in peace and quiet.

I had assuredly witnessed a new thing on that unpromising day, something quite different from anything witnessed in my wide rambles; and, though a little thing, it had been a most entertaining comedy in bird life with a very proper ending. It was clear that the sick blackbird had bitterly resented the treatment he had received; that, brooding on it out in the cold, his anger had made him strong, and that he came back determined to fight, with his plan of action matured. He was not going to be made a fool every time!

The birds all gone their several ways at last, I got up from my stone and wondered if the old Romans ever dreamed that this wall which they made to endure would after seventeen hundred years have no more important use than this – to afford shelter to a few little birds and to the solitary man that watched them from the bleak wind. Many a strange Roman curse on this ungenial climate must these same stones have heard.

Looking through a gap in the wall I saw, close by, on the other side, a dozen men at work with pick and shovel throwing up huge piles of earth. They were uncovering a small portion of that ancient buried city and were finding the foundations and floors and hypocausts of Silchester's public baths; also some broken pottery and trifling ornaments of bronze and bone. The workmen in that bitter wind were decidedly better off than the gentlemen from Burlington House in charge of the excavations. These stood with coats buttoned up and hands thrust deep down in their pockets. It seemed to me that it was better to sit in the shelter of the wall and watch the birds than to burrow in the crumbling dust for that small harvest. Yet I could understand and even appreciate their work, although it is probable that the glow I experienced was in part reflected. Perhaps my mental attitude, when standing in that sheltered place, and when getting on to the windy wall I looked down on the workers and their work, was merely benevolent. I had pleasure in their pleasure, and a vague desire for a better understanding, a closer alliance and harmony. It was the desire that we might all see nature – the globe with all it contains – as one harmonious whole, not as groups of things, or phenomena, unrelated, cast there by chance or by careless or contemptuous gods. This dust of past ages, dug out of a wheat-field, with its fragments of men's work – its pottery and tiles and stones – this is a part, too, even as the small birds, with their little motives and passions, so like man's, are a part. I thought with self shame of my own sins in this connection; then, considering the lesser faults on the other side, I wished that Mr. St. John Hope would experience a like softening mood and regret that he had abused the ivy. It grieves me to hear it called a 'noxious weed.' That perished people, whose remains in this land so deeply interest him, were the mightiest 'builders of ruins' the world has known; but who except the archaeologist would wish to see these piled stones in their naked harshness, striking the mind with dismay at the thought of Time and its perpetual desolations! I like better the old Spanish poet who says, 'What of Rome; its world-conquering power, and majesty and glory – what has it come to?' The ivy on the wall, the yellow wallflower, tell it. A 'deadly parasite' quotha! Is it not well that this plant, this evergreen tapestry of innumerable leaves, should cover and partly hide and partly reveal the 'strange defeatures' the centuries have set on man's greatest works? I would have no ruin nor no old and noble building without it; for not only does it beautify decay, but from long association it has come to be in the mind a very part of such scenes and so interwoven with the human tragedy, that, like the churchyard yew, it seems the most human of green things.

Here in September great masses of the plant are already showing a greenish cream-colour of the opening blossoms, which will be at their perfection in October. Then, when the sun shines, there will be no lingering red admiral, nor blue fly or fly of any colour, nor yellow wasp, nor any honey-eating or late honey-gathering insect that will not be here to feed on the ivy's sweetness. And behind the blossoming curtain, alive with the minute, multitudinous, swift-moving, glittering forms, some nobler form will be hidden in a hole or fissure in the wall. Here on many a night I have listened to the sibilant screech of the white owl and the brown owl's clear, long-drawn, quavering lamentation:

'Good Ivy, what byrdys hast thou?'
'Non but the Howlet, that How! How!'

CHAPTER NINE

Rural Rides

'A-birding on a Broncho' is the title of a charming little book published some years ago, and probably better known to readers on the other side of the Atlantic than in England. I remember reading it with pleasure and pride on account of the author's name, Florence Merriam, seeing that, on my mother's side, I am partly a Merriam myself (of the branch on the other side of the Atlantic), and having been informed that all of that rare name are of one family, I took it that we were related, though perhaps very distantly. 'A-birding on a Broncho' suggested an equally alliterative title for this chapter – 'Birding on a Bike'; but I will leave it to others, for those who go a-birding are now very many and are hard put to find fresh titles to their books. For several reasons it will suit me better to borrow from Cobbett and name this chapter 'Rural Rides.'

Some of us do not go out on bicycles to observe the ways of birds. Indeed, some of our common species have grown almost too familiar with the wheel: it has become a positive danger to them. They not infrequently mistake its rate of speed and injure themselves in attempting to fly across it. Recently I had a thrush knock himself senseless against the spokes of my forewheel, and cycling friends have told me of similar experiences they have had, in some instances the heedless birds getting killed. Chaffinches are like the children in village streets – they will not get out of your way; by and by in rural places the merciful man will have to ring his bell almost incessantly to avoid running over them. As I do not travel at a furious speed I manage to avoid most things, even the wandering loveless oil-beetle and the small rose-beetle and that slow-moving insect tortoise the tumble-dung. Two or three seasons ago I was so unfortunate as to run over a large and beautifully bright grass snake near Aldermaston, once a snake sanctuary. He writhed and wriggled on the road as if I had broken his back, but on picking him up I was pleased to find that my wind-inflated rubber tyre had not, like the brazen chariot wheel, crushed his delicate vertebrae; he quickly recovered, and when released glided swiftly and easily away into cover. Twice only have I deliberately tried to run down, to tread on coat-tails so to speak, of any wild creature. One was a weasel, the other a stoat, running along at a hedge-side before me. In both instances, just as the front wheel was touching the tail, the little flat-headed rascal swerved quickly aside and escaped.

Even some of the less common and less tame birds care as little for a man on a bicycle as they do for a cow. Not long ago a peewit trotted leisurely across the road not more than ten yards from my front wheel; and on the same day I came upon a green woodpecker enjoying a dust-bath in the public road. He declined to stir until I stopped to watch him, then merely flew about a dozen yards away and attached himself to the trunk of a fir tree at the roadside and waited there for me to go. Never in all my wanderings afoot had I seen a yaffingale dusting himself like a barn-door fowl!

It is not seriously contended that birds can be observed narrowly in this easy way; but even for the most conscientious field naturalist the wheel has its advantages. It carries him quickly over much barren ground and gives him a better view of the country he traverses; finally, it enables him to see more birds. He will sometimes see thousands in a day where, walking, he would hardly have seen hundreds, and there is joy in mere numbers. It was just to get this general rapid sight of the bird life of the neighbouring hilly district of Hampshire that I was at Newbury on the last day of October. The weather was bright though very cold and windy, and towards evening I was surprised to see about twenty swallows in Northbrook Street flying languidly to and fro in the shelter of the houses, often fluttering under the eaves and at intervals sitting on ledges and projections. These belated birds looked as if they wished to hibernate, or find the most cosy holes to die in, rather than to emigrate. On the following day at noon they came out again and flew up and down in the same feeble aimless manner.

Undoubtedly a few swallows of all three species, but mostly house-martins, do 'lie up' in England every winter, but probably very few survive to the following spring. We should have said that it was impossible that any should survive but for one authentic instance in recent years, in which a barn-swallow lived through the winter in a semi-torpid state in an outhouse at a country vicarage. What came of the Newbury birds I do not know, as I left on the 2nd of November – tore myself away, I may say, for, besides meeting with people I didn't know who treated a stranger with sweet friendliness, it is a town which quickly wins one's affections. It is built of bricks of a good deep rich red – not the painfully bright red so much in use now – and no person has had the bad taste to spoil the harmony by introducing stone and stucco. Moreover, Newbury has, in Shaw House, an Elizabethan mansion of the rarest beauty. Let him that is weary of the ugliness and discords in our town buildings go and stand by the ancient cedar at the gate and look across the wide green lawn at this restful house, subdued by time to a tender rosy-red colour on its walls and a deep dark red on its roof, clouded with grey of lichen.

From Newbury and the green meadows of the Kennet the Hampshire hills may be seen, looking like the South Down range at its highest point viewed from the Sussex Weald. I made for Coombe Hill, the highest hill in Hampshire, and found it a considerable labour to push my machine up from the pretty tree-hidden village of East Woodhay at its foot. The top is a league-long tableland, with stretches of green elastic turf, thickets of furze and bramble, and clumps of ancient noble beeches – a beautiful lonely wilderness with rabbits and birds for only inhabitants. From the highest point where a famous gibbet stands for ever a thousand feet above the sea and where there is a dew-pond, the highest in England, which has never dried up although a large flock of sheep drink in it every summer day, one looks down into an immense hollow, a Devil's Punch Bowl very many times magnified, – and spies, far away and far below, a few lonely houses half hidden by trees at the bottom. This is the romantic village of Coombe, and hither I went and found the vicar busy in the garden of the small old picturesque parsonage. Here a very pretty little bird comedy was in progress: a pair of stock-doves which had been taken from a rabbit-hole in the hill and reared by hand had just escaped from the large cage where they had always lived, and all the family were excitedly engaged in trying to recapture them. They were delightful to see – those two pretty blue birds with red legs running busily about on the green lawn, eagerly searching for something to eat and finding nothing. They were quite tame and willing to be fed, so that anyone could approach them and put as much salt on their tails as he liked, but they refused to be touched or taken; they were too happy in their new freedom, running and flying about in that brilliant sunshine, and when I left towards the evening they were still at large.

But before quitting that small isolated village in its green basin – a human heart in a chalk hill, almost the highest in England – I wished the hours I spent in it had been days, so much was there to see and hear. There was the gibbet on the hill, for example, far up on the rim of the green basin, four hundred feet above the village; why had that memorial, that symbol of a dreadful past, been preserved for so many years and generations? and why had it been raised so high – was it because the crime of the person put to death there was of so monstrous a nature that it was determined to suspend him, if not on a gibbet fifty cubits high, at all events higher above the earth than Haman the son of Hammedatha the Agagite? The gruesome story is as follows.

Once upon a time there lived a poor widow woman in Coombe, with two sons, aged fourteen and sixteen, who worked at a farm in the village. She had a lover, a middle-aged man, living at Woodhay, a carrier who used to go on two or three days each week with his cart to deliver parcels at Coombe. But he was a married man, and as he could not marry the widow while his wife remained alive, it came into his dull Berkshire brain that the only way out of the difficulty was to murder her, and to this course the widow probably consented. Accordingly, one day, he invited or persuaded her to accompany him on his journey to the remote village, and on the way he got her out of the cart and led her into a close thicket to show her something he had discovered there. What he wished to show her (according to one version of the story) was a populous hornets' nest, and having got her there he suddenly flung her against it and made off, leaving the cloud of infuriated hornets to sting her to death. That night he slept at Coombe, or stayed till a very late hour at the widow's cottage and told her what he had done. In telling her he had spoken in his ordinary voice, but by and by it occurred to him that the two boys, who were sleeping close by in the living-room, might have been awake and listening. She assured him that they were both fast asleep, but he was not satisfied, and said that if they had heard him he would kill them both, as he had no wish to swing, and he could not trust them to hold their tongues. Thereupon they got up and examined the faces of the two boys, holding a candle over them, and saw that they were in a deep sleep, as was natural after their long day's hard work on the farm, and the murderer's fears were set at rest. Yet one of the boys, the younger, had been wide awake all the time, listening, trembling with terror, with wide eyes to the dreadful tale, and only when they first became suspicious instinct came to his aid and closed his eyes and stilled his tremors and gave him the appearance of being asleep. Early next morning, with his terror still on him, he told what he had heard to his brother, and by and by, unable to keep the dreadful secret, they related it to someone – a carter or ploughman on the farm. He in turn told the farmer, who at once gave information, and in a short time the man and woman were arrested. In due time they were tried, convicted, and sentenced to be hanged in the parish where the crime had been committed.

Everybody was delighted, and Coombe most delighted of all, for it happened that some of their wise people had been diligently examining into the matter and had made the discovery that the woman had been murdered just outside their borders in the adjoining parish of Inkpen, so that they were going to enjoy seeing the wicked punished at somebody else's expense. Inkpen was furious and swore that it would not be saddled with the cost of a great public double execution. The line dividing the two parishes had always been a doubtful one; now they were going to take the benefit of the doubt and let Coombe hang its own miscreants!

As neither side would yield, the higher authorities were compelled to settle the matter for them, and ordered the cost to be divided between the two parishes, the gibbet to be erected on the boundary line, as far as it could be ascertained. This was accordingly done, the gibbet being erected at the highest point crossed by the line, on a stretch of beautiful smooth elastic turf, among prehistoric earthworks – a spot commanding one of the finest and most extensive views in Southern England. The day appointed for the execution brought the greatest concourse of people ever witnessed at that lofty spot, at all events since prehistoric times. If some of the ancient Britons had come out of their graves to look on, seated on their earthworks, they would have probably rubbed their ghostly hands together and remarked to each other that it reminded them of old times. All classes were there, from the nobility and gentry, on horseback and in great coaches in which they carried their own provisions, to the meaner sort who had trudged from all the country round on foot, and those who had not brought their own food and beer were catered for by traders in carts. The crowd was a hilarious one, and no doubt that grand picnic on the beacon was the talk of they country for a generation or longer. The two wretches having been hanged in chains on one gibbet were left to be eaten by ravens, crows, and magpipes, and dried by sun and winds, until, after long years, the swinging, creaking skeletons with their chains on fell to pieces and were covered with the turf, but the gibbet itself was never removed.

Then a strange thing happened. The sheep on a neighbouring farm became thin and sickly and yielded little wool and died before their time. No remedies availed and the secret of their malady could not be discovered; but it went on so long that the farmer was threatened with utter ruin. Then, by chance, it was discovered that the chains in which the murderers had been hanged had been thrown by some evil-minded person into a dew-pond on the farm. This was taken to be the cause of the malady in the sheep; at all events, the chains having been taken out of the pond and buried deep in the earth, the flock recovered: it was supposed that the person who had thrown the chains in the water to poison it had done so to ruin the farmer in revenge for some injustice or grudge.

But even now we are not quite done with the gibbet! Many, many years had gone by when Inkpen discovered from old documents that their little dishonest neighbour, Coombe, had taken more land than she was entitled to, that not only a part but the whole of that noble hill-top belonged to her! It was Inkpen's turn to chuckle now; but she chuckled too soon, and Coombe, running out to look, found the old rotten stump of the gibbet still in the ground. Hands off! she cried. Here stands a post, which you set up yourself, or which we put up together and agreed that this should be the boundary line for ever. Inkpen sneaked off to hide herself in her village, and Coombe, determined to keep the subject in mind, set up a brand-new stout gibbet in the place of the old rotting one. That too decayed and fell to pieces in time, and the present gibbet is therefore the third, and nobody has ever been hanged on it. Coombe is rather proud of it, but I am not sure that Inkpen is.

That was one of three strange events in the life of the village which I heard: the other two must be passed by; they would take long to tell and require a good pen to do them justice. To me the best thing in or of the village was the vicar himself, my put-upon host, a man of so blithe a nature, so human and companionable, that when I, a perfect stranger without an introduction or any excuse for such intrusion, came down like a wolf on his luncheon-table, he received me as if I had been an old friend or one of his own kindred, and freely gave up his time to me for the rest of that day. To count his years he was old: he had been vicar of Coombe for half a century, but he was a young man still and had never had a day's illness in his life – he did not know what a headache was. He smoked with me, and to prove that he was not a total abstainer he drank my health in a glass of port wine – very good wine. It was Coombe that did it – its peaceful life, isolated from a distracting world in that hollow hill, and the marvellous purity of its air. 'Sitting there on my lawn,' he said, 'you are six hundred feet above the sea, although in a hollow four hundred feet deep.' It was an ideal open-air room, round and green, with the sky for a roof. In winter it was sometimes very cold, and after a heavy fall of snow the scene was strange and impressive from the tiny village set in its stupendous dazzling white bowl. Not only on those rare arctic days, but at all times it was wonderfully quiet. The shout of a child or the peaceful crow of a cock was the loudest sound you heard. Once a gentleman from London town came down to spend a week at the parsonage. Towards evening on the very first day he grew restless and complained of the abnormal stillness. 'I like a quiet place well enough,' he exclaimed, 'but this tingling silence I can't stand!' And stand it he wouldn't and didn't, for on the very next morning he took himself off. Many years had gone by, but the vicar could not forget the Londoner who had come down to invent a new way of describing the Coombe silence. His tingling phrase was a joy for ever.

He took me to the church – one of the tiniest churches in the country, just the right size for a church in a tiny village and assured me that he had never once locked the door in his fifty years – day and night it was open to anyone to enter. It was a refuge and shelter from the storm and the Tempest, and many a poor homeless wretch had found a dry place to sleep in that church during the last half a century. This man's feeling of pity and tenderness for the very poor, even the outcast and tramp, was a passion. But how strange all this would sound in the ears of many country clergymen! How many have told me when I have gone to the parsonage to 'borrow the key' that it had been found necessary to keep the church door locked, to prevent damage, thefts, etc. 'Have *you* never had anything stolen?' I asked him. Yes, once, a great many years ago, the church plate had been taken away in the night. But it was recovered: the thief had taken it to the top of the hill and thrown it into the dewpond there, no doubt intending to take it out and dispose of it at some more convenient time. But it was found, and had ever since then been kept safe at the vicarage. Nothing of value to tempt a man to steal was kept in the church. *He* had never locked it, but once in his fifty years it had been locked against him by the churchwardens. This happened in the days of the Joseph Arch agitation, when the agricultural labourer's condition was being hotly discussed throughout the country. The vicar's heart was stirred, for he knew better than most how hard these conditions were at Coombe and in the surrounding parishes. He took up the subject and preached on it in his own pulpit in a way that offended the landowners and alarmed the farmers in the district. The church wardens, who were farmers, then locked him out of his church, and for two or three weeks there was no public worship in the parish of Coombe. Doubtless their action was applauded by all the substantial men in the neighbourhood; the others who lived in the cottages and were unsubstantial didn't matter. That storm blew over, but its conse-quences endured, one being that the inflammatory parson continued to be regarded with cold disapproval by the squires and their larger tenants. But the vicar himself was unrepentant and unashamed; on the contrary, he gloried in what he had said and done, and was proud to be able to relate that a quarter of a century later one of the two men who had taken that extreme course said to him, 'We locked you out of your own church, but years have brought me to another mind about that question. I see it in a different light now and know that you were right and we were wrong.'

Towards evening I said good-bye to my kind friend and entertainer and continued my rural ride. From Coombe it is five miles to Hurst-bourne Tarrant, another charming 'highland' village, and the road, sloping down the entire distance, struck me as one of the best to be on I had travelled in Hampshire, running along a narrow green valley, with oak and birch and bramble and thorn in their late autumn colours growing on the slopes on either hand. Probably the beauty of the scene, or the swift succession of beautiful scenes, with the low sun flaming on the 'coloured shades,' served to keep out of my mind something that should have been in it. At all events, it was odd that I had more than once promised myself a visit to the very village I was approaching solely because William Cobbett had described and often stayed in it, and now no thought of him and his ever-delightful *Rural Rides* was in my mind.

Arrived at the village I went straight to the 'George and Dragon,' where a friend had assured me I could always find good accommoda-tion. But he was wrong: there was no room for me, I was told by a weird-looking, lean, white-haired old woman with whity-blue unfriendly eyes. She appeared to resent it that any one should ask for accommodation at such a time, when the 'shooting gents' from town required all the rooms available. Well, I had to sleep somewhere, I told her: couldn't she direct me to a cottage where I could get a bed? No, she couldn't – it is always so; but after the third time of asking she unfroze so far as to say that perhaps they would take me in at a cottage close by. So I went, and a poor kind widow who lived there with a son consented to put me up. She made a nice fire in the sitting-room, and after warming myself before it, while watching the firelight and shadows playing on the dim walls and ceiling, it came to me that I was not in a cottage, but in a large room with an oak floor and wainscoting. 'Do you call this a cottage?' I said to the woman when she came in with tea. 'No, I have it as a cottage, but it is an old farm-house called the Rookery,' she returned. Then, for the first time, I remembered *Rural Rides*. 'This then is the very house where William Cobbett used to stay seventy or eighty years ago,' I said. She had never heard of William Cobbett; she only knew that at that date it had been tenanted by a farmer named Blount, a Roman Catholic, who had some curious ideas about the land.

That settled it. Blount was the name of Cobbett's friend, and I had come to the very house where Cobbett was accustomed to stay. But how odd that my first thought of the man should have come to me when sitting by the fire where Cobbett himself had sat on many a cold evening! And this was November the second, the very day eighty-odd years ago when he paid his first visit to the Rookery; at all events, it is the first date he gives in *Rural Rides*. And he too had been delighted with the place and the beauty of the surrounding country with the trees in their late autumn colours. Writing on November 2nd, 1821, he says: 'The place is commonly called Uphusband, which is, I think, as decent a corruption of names as one could wish to meet with. However, Uphusband the people will have it, and Uphusband it shall be for me.' That is indeed how he names it all through his book, after explaining that 'husband' is a corruption of Hurstbourne, and that there are two Hurstbournes, this being the upper one.

I congratulated myself on having been refused accommodation at the 'George and Dragon,' and was more than satisfied to pass an evening without a book, sitting there alone listening to an imaginary conversation between those two curious friends. 'Lord Carnarvon,' says Cobbett, 'told a man, in 1820, that *he did not like my politics*. But what did he mean by my *politics*? I have no politics but such as he *ought* to like. To be sure I labour most assiduously to destroy a system of distress and misery; but is that any reason why a Lord should dislike my politics? However, dislike them or like them, to them, to those very politics, the Lords themselves *must come at last*.'

Undoubtedly he talked like that, just as he wrote and as he spoke in public, his style, if style it can be called, being the most simple, direct, and colloquial ever written. And for this reason, when we are aweary of the style of the stylist, where the living breathing body becomes of less consequence than its beautiful clothing, it is a relief, and refreshment, to turn from the precious and delicate expression, the implicit word, sought for high and low and at last found, the balance of every sentence and perfect harmony of the whole work – to go from it to the simple vigorous unadorned talk of *Rural Rides*. A classic, and as incongruous among classics as a farmer in his smock-frock, leggings, and stout boots would appear in a company of fine gentlemen in fashionable dress. The powerful face is the main thing, and we think little of the frock and leggings and how the hair is parted or if parted at all. Harsh and crabbed as his nature no doubt was, and bitter and spiteful at times, his conversation must yet have seemed like a perpetual feast of honeyed sweets to his farmer friend. Doubtless there was plenty of variety in it: now he would expatiate on the beauty of the green downs over which he had just ridden, the wooded slopes in their glorious autumn colours, and the rich villages between; this would remind him of Malthus, that blasphemous monster who had dared to say that the increase in food production did not keep pace with increase of population; then a quieting down, a breathing-space, all about the turnip crop, the price of eggs at Weyhill Fair, and the delights of hare coursing, until politics would come round again and a fresh outburst from the glorious demagogue in his tantrums.

At eight o'clock Cobbett would say good night and go to bed, and early next morning write down what he had said to his friend, or some of it, and send it off to be printed in his paper. That, I take it, is how *Rural Rides* was written, and that is why it seems so fresh to us to this day, and that to take it up after other books is like going out from a luxurious room full of fine company into the open air to feel the wind and rain on one's face and see the green grass.

But I very much regret that Cobbett tells us nothing of his farmer friend. Blount, I imagine, must have been a man of a very fine character to have won the heart and influenced such a person. Cobbett never loses an opportunity of vilifying the parsons and expressing his hatred of the Established Church; and yet, albeit a Protestant, he invariably softens down when he refers to the Roman Catholic faith and appears quite capable of seeing the good that is in it. It was Blount, I think, who had soothed the savage breast of the man in this matter. The only thing I could hear about Blount and his 'queer notions' regarding the land was his idea that the soil could be improved by taking the flints out. 'The soil to look upon,' Cobbett truly says, 'appears to be more than half flint, but is a very good quality.' Blount thought to make it better, and for many years employed all the aged poor villagers and the children in picking the flints from the ploughed land and gathering them in vast heaps. It does not appear that he made his land more productive, but his hobby was a good one for the poor of the village; the stones, too, proved useful afterwards to the road-makers, who have been using them these many years. A few heaps almost clothed over with a turf which had formed on them in the course of eighty years were still to be seen on the land when I was there.

The following day I took no ride. The weather was so beautiful it seemed better to spend the time sitting or basking in the warmth and brightness or strolling about. At all events, it was a perfect day at Hurstbourne Tarrant, though not everywhere, for on that third of November the greatest portion of Southern England was drowned in a cold dense white fog. In London it was dark, I heard. Early in the morning I listened to a cirl bunting singing merrily from a bush close to the 'George and Dragon' Inn. This charming bird is quite common in the neighbourhood, although, as elsewhere in England, the natives know it not by its book name, nor by any other, and do not distinguish it from its less engaging cousin, the yellowhammer.

After breakfast I strolled about the common and in Doles Wood, on the down above the village, listening to the birds, and on my way back encountered a tramp whose singular appearance produced a deep impression on my mind. We have heard of a work by some modest pressman entitled 'Monarchs I have met', and I sometimes think that one equally interesting might be written on 'Tramps I have met'. As I have neither time nor stomach for the task, I will make a present of the title to any one of my fellow-travellers, curious in tramps, who cares to use it. This makes two good titles I have given away in this chapter with a borrowed one.

But if it had been possible for me to write such a book, a prominent place would be given in it to the one tramp I have met who could be accurately described as *gorgeous*. I did not cultivate his acquaintance; chance threw us together and we separated after exchanging a few polite commonplaces, but his big flamboyant image remains vividly impressed on my mind.

At noon, in the brilliant sunshine, as I came loiteringly down the long slope from Doles Wood to the village, he overtook me. He was a huge man, over six feet high, nobly built, suggesting a Scandinavian origin, with a broad blond face, good features, and prominent blue eyes, and his hair was curly and shone like gold in the sunlight. Had he been a mere labourer in a workman's rough clay-stained clothes, one would have stood still to look at and admire him, and say perhaps what a magnificent warrior he would have looked with sword and spear and plumed helmet, mounted on a big horse! But alas! he had the stamp of the irreclaimable blackguard on his face; and that same handsome face was just then disfigured with several bruises in three colours – blue, black, and red. Doubtless he had been in a drunken brawl on the previous evening and had perhaps been thrown out of some low public-house and properly punished.

In his dress he was as remarkable as in his figure. Bright blue trousers much too small for his stout legs, once the property, no doubt, of some sporting young gent of loud tastes in colours; a spotted fancy waistcoat, not long enough to meet the trousers, a dirty scarlet tie, long black frock-coat, shiny in places, and a small dirty grey cap which only covered the topmost part of his head of golden hair.

Walking by the hedge-side he picked and devoured the late blackberries, which were still abundant. It was a beautiful unkept hedge with scarlet and purple fruit among the many-coloured fading leaves and silver-grey down of old-man's-beard.

I too picked and ate a few berries and made the remark that it was late to eat such fruit in November. The Devil in these parts, I told him, flies abroad in October to spit on the bramble bushes and spoil the fruit. It was even worse further north, in Norfolk and Suffolk, where they say the Devil goes out at Michaelmas and shakes his verminous trousers over the bushes.

He didn't smile; he went on sternly eating blackberries, and then remarked in a bitter tone, 'That Devil they talk about must have a busy time, to go messing about blackberry bushes in addition to all his other important work.'

I was silent, and presently, after swallowing a few more berries, he resumed in the same tone: 'Very fine, very beautiful all this' – waving his hand to indicate the hedge, its rich tangle of purple-red stems and coloured leaves, and scarlet fruit and silvery old-man's-beard. 'An artist enjoys seeing this sort of thing, and it's nice for all those who go about just for the pleasure of seeing things. But when it comes to a man tramping twenty or thirty miles a day on an empty belly, looking for work which he can't find, he doesn't see it quite in the same way.'

'True,' I returned, with indifference.

But he was not to be put off by my sudden coldness, and he proceeded to inform me that he had just returned from Salisbury Plain, that it had been noised abroad that ten thousand men were wanted by the War Office to work in forming new camps. On arrival he found it was not so – it was all a lie – men were not wanted – and he was now on his way to Andover, penniless and hungry and –

By the time he had got to that part of his story we were some distance apart, as I had remained standing still while he, thinking me still close behind, had gone on picking blackberries and talking. He was soon out of sight.

At noon the following day, the weather still being bright and genial, I went to Crux Easton, a hilltop village consisting of some low farm buildings, cottages, and a church not much bigger than a cottage. A great house probably once existed here, as the hill has a noble avenue of limes, which it wears like a comb or crest. On the lower slope of the hill, the old unkept hedges were richer in colour than in most places, owing to the abundance of the spindle-wood tree, laden with its loose clusters of flame-bright, purple-pink and orange berries.

Here I saw a pretty thing: a cock cirl bunting, his yellow breast towards me, sitting quietly on a large bush of these same brilliant berries, set amidst a mass of splendidly coloured hazel leaves, mixed with bramble and tangled with ivy and silver-grey traveller's-joy. An artist's heart would have leaped with joy at the sight, but all his skill and oriental colours would have made nothing of it, for all visible nature was part of the picture, the wide wooded earth and the blue sky beyond and above the bird, and the sunshine that glorified all.

On the other side of the hedge there were groups of fine old beech trees and, strange to see, just beyond the green slope and coloured trees, was the great whiteness of the fog which had advanced thus far and now appeared motionless. I went down and walked by the side of the bank of mist, feeling its clammy coldness on one cheek while the other was fanned by the warm bright air. Seen at a distance of a couple of hundred yards, the appearance was that of a beautiful pearly-white cloud resting upon the earth. Many fogs had I seen, but never one like this, so substantial-looking, so sharply defined, standing like a vast white wall or flat-topped hill at the foot of the green sunlit slope! I had the fancy that if I had been an artist in sculpture, and rapid modeller, by using the edge of my hand as a knife I could have roughly carved out a human figure, then drawing it gently out of the mass proceeded to press and work it to a better shape, the shape, let us say, of a beautiful woman. Then, if it were done excellently, and some man-mocking deity, or power of the air, happened to be looking on, he would breathe life and intelligence into it, and send it, or her, abroad to mix with human kind and complicate their affairs. For she would seem a woman and would be like some women we have known, beautiful with blue flower-like eyes, pale gold or honey-coloured hair; very white of skin, Leightonian, almost diaphanous, so delicate as to make all other skins appear coarse and made of clay. And with her beauty and a mysterious sweetness not of the heart, since no heart there would be in that mist-cold body, she would draw all hearts, ever inspiring, but never satisfying passion, her beauty and alluring smiles being but the brightness of a cloud on which the sun is shining.

Birds, driven by the fog to that sunlit spot, were all about me in incredible numbers. Rooks and daws were congregating on the bushes, where their black figures served to intensify the red-gold tints of the foliage. At intervals the entire vast cawing multitude simultaneously rose up with a sound as of many waters, and appeared now at last about to mount up into the blue heavens, to float circling there far above the world as they are accustomed to do on warm windless days in autumn. But in a little while their brave note would change to one of trouble; the sight of that immeasurable whiteness covering so much of the earth would scare them, and led by hundreds of clamouring daws they would come down again to settle once more in black masses on the shining yellow trees.

Close by a ploughed field of about forty acres was the camping-ground of an army of peewits; they were travellers from the north perhaps, and were quietly resting, sprinkled over the whole area. More abundant were the small birds in mixed flocks or hordes – finches, buntings, and larks in thousands on thousands, with a sprinkling of pipits and pied and grey wagtails, all busily feeding on the stubble and fresh ploughed land. Thickly and evenly distributed, they appeared to the vision ranging over the brown level expanse as minute animated and variously coloured clods – black and brown and grey and yellow and olive-green.

It was a rare pleasure to be in this company, to revel in their astonishing numbers, to feast my soul on them as it were – little birds in such multitudes that ten thousand Frenchmen and Italians might have gorged to repletion on their small succulent bodies – and to reflect that they were safe from persecution so long as they remained here in England. This is something for an Englishman to be proud of.

After spending two hours at Crux Easton, with that dense immovable fog close by, I at length took the plunge to get to Highclere. What a change! I was at once where all form and colour and melody had been blotted out. My clothes were hoary with clinging mist, my fingers numb with cold, and Highclere, its scattered cottages appearing like dim smudges through the whiteness, was the dreariest village on earth. I fled on to Newbury in quest of warmth and light, and found it indoors, but the town was deep in the fog.

The next day I ventured out again to look for the sun, and found it not, but my ramble was not without its reward. In a pine wood three miles from the town I stood awhile to listen to the sound as of copious rain of the moisture dropping from the trees, when a sudden tempest of loud, sharp metallic notes – a sound dear to the ornithologist's ears – made me jump; and down into the very tree before which I was standing dropped a flock of about twenty crossbills. So excited and noisy when coming down, the instant they touched the tree they became perfectly silent and motionless. Seven of their number had settled on the outside shoots, and sat there within forty feet of me, looking like painted wooden images of small green and greenish-yellow parrots; for a space of fifteen minutes not the slightest movement did they make, and at length, before going, I waved my arms about and shouted to frighten them, and still they refused to stir.

Next morning that memorable fog lifted, to England's joy, and quitting my refuge I went out once more into the region of high sheep-walks, adorned with beechen woods and traveller's-joy in the hedges, rambling by Highclere, Burghclere, and Kingsclere. The last – Hampshire's little Cuzco – is a small and village-like old red brick town, unapproached by a railroad and unimproved, therefore still beautiful, as were all places in other, better, less civilized days. Here in the late afternoon a chilly grey haze crept over the country and set me wishing for a fireside and the sound of friendly voices, and I turned my face towards beloved Silchester. Leaving the hills behind me I got away from the haze and went my devious way by serpentine roads through a beautiful, wooded, undulating country. And I wish that for a hundred, nay, for a thousand years to come, I could on each recurring November have such an afternoon ride, with that autumnal glory in the trees. Sometimes, seeing the road before me carpeted with pure yellow, I said to myself, now I am coming to elms; but when the road shone red and russet-gold before me I knew it was overhung by beeches. But the oak is the common tree in this place, and from every high point on the road I saw far before me and on either hand the woods and copses all a tawny yellow gold – the hue of the dying oak leaf. The tall larches were lemon-yellow, and when growing among tall pines produced a singular effect. Best of all was it where beeches grew among the firs, and the low sun on my left hand shining through the wood gave the coloured translucent leaves an unimaginable splendour. This was the very effect which men, inspired by a sacred passion, had sought to reproduce in their noblest work – the Gothic cathedral and church, its dim interior lit by many-coloured stained glass. The only choristers in these natural fanes were the robins and the small lyrical wren; but on passing through the rustic village of Wolverton I stopped for a couple of minutes to listen to the lively strains of a cirl bunting among some farm buildings.

Then on to Silchester, its furzy common and scattered village and the vast ruinous walls, overgrown with ivy, bramble, and thorn, of ancient Roman Calleva. Inside the walls, at one spot, a dozen men were still at work in the fading light; they were just finishing – shovelling earth in to obliterate all that had been opened out during the year. The old flint foundations that had been revealed; the houses with porches and corridors and courtyards and pillared hypocausts; the winter room with its wide beautiful floor – red and black and white and grey and yellow, with geometric pattern and twist and scroll and flower and leaf and quaint figures of man and beast and bird – all to be covered up with earth so that the plough may be driven over it again, and the wheat grow and ripen again as it has grown and ripened there above the dead city for so many centuries. The very earth within those walls had a reddish cast owing to the innumerable fragments of red tile and tessera mixed with it. Larks and finches were busily searching for seeds in the reddish-brown soil. They would soon be gone to their roosting-places and the tired men to their cottages, and the white owl coming from his hiding-place in the walls would have old Silchester to himself, as he has had it since the cries and moans of the conquered died into silence so long ago.

CHAPTER TEN

The Last of His Name

I came by chance to the village – Norton, we will call it, just to call it something, but the county in which it is situated need not be named. It happened that about noon that day I planned to pass the night at a village where, as I was informed at a small country town I had rested in, there was a nice inn – 'The Fox and Grapes' – to put up at, but when I arrived, tired and hungry, I was told that I could not have a bed and that the only thing to do was to try Norton, which also boasted an inn. It was hard to have to turn some two or three miles out of my road at that late hour on a chance of a shelter for the night, but there was nothing else to do, so on to Norton I went with heavy steps, and arrived a little after sunset, more tired and hungry than ever, only to be told at the inn that they had no accommodation for me, that their one spare room had been engaged! 'What am I to do, then?' I demanded of the landlord. 'Beyond this village I cannot go to-night – do you want me to go out and sleep under a hedge?' He called his spouse, and after some conversation they said the village baker might be able to put me up, as he had a spare bedroom in his house. So to the baker's I went, and found it a queer, ramshackle old place, standing a little back from the village street in a garden and green plot with a few fruit trees growing on it. To my knock the baker himself came out – a mild-looking, flabby-faced man, with his mouth full, in a very loose suit of pyjama-like garments of a bluish floury colour. I told him my story, and he listened, swallowing his mouthful, then cast his eyes down and rubbed his chin, which had a small tuft of hairs growing on it, and finally said, 'I don't know. I must ask my wife. But come in and have a cup of tea – we're just having a cup ourselves, and perhaps you'd like one.'

I could have told him that I should like a dozen cups and a great many slices of bread-and-butter, if there was nothing else more substantial to be had. However, I only said, 'Thank you,' and followed him in to where his wife, a nice-looking woman, with black hair and olive face, was seated behind the teapot. Imagine my surprise when I found that besides tea there was a big hot repast on the table – a ham, a roast fowl, potatoes and cabbage, a rice pudding, a dish of stewed fruit, bread-and-butter, and other things!

'You call this a cup of tea!' I exclaimed delightedly. The woman laughed, and he explained in an apologetic way that he had formerly suffered grievously from indigestion, so that for many years his life was a burden to him, until he discovered that if he took one big meal a day, after the work was over, he could keep perfectly well.

I was never hungrier than on this evening, and never, I think, ate a bigger or more enjoyable meal; nor have I ever ceased to remember those two with gratitude, and if I were to tell here what they told me – the history of their two lives – I think it would be a more interesting story than the one I am about to relate. I stayed a whole week in their hospitable house; a week which passed only too quickly, for never had I been in a sweeter haunt of peace than this village in a quiet, green country remote from towns and stations. It was a small rustic place, a few old houses and thatched cottages, and the ancient church with square Norman tower hard to see amid the immense old oaks and elms that grew all about it. At the end of the village were the park gates, and the park, a solitary, green place with noble trees, was my favourite haunt; for there was no one to forbid me, the squire being dead, the old red Elizabethan house empty, with only a caretaker in the gardener's lodge to mind it, and the estate for sale. Three years it had been in that condition, but nobody seemed to want it; occasionally some important person came rushing down in a motor-car, but after running over the house he would come out and, remarking that it was a 'rummy old place,' remount his car and vanish in a cloud of dust to be seen no more.

The dead owner, I found, was much in the village mind; and no wonder, since Norton had never been without a squire until he passed away, leaving no one to succeed him. It was as if some ancient land-mark, or an immemorial oak tree on the green in whose shade the villagers had been accustomed to sit for many generations, had been removed. There was a sense of something wanting something gone out of their lives. Moreover, he had been a man of a remarkable character, and though they never loved him they yet reverenced his memory.

So much was he in their minds that I could not be in the village and not hear the story of his life – the story which, I said, interested me less than that of the good baker and his wife. On his father's death at a very advanced age he came, a comparative stranger, to Norton, the first half of his life having been spent abroad. He was then a middle-aged man, unmarried, and a bachelor he remained to the end. He was of a reticent disposition and was said to be proud; formal, almost cold, in manner; furthermore, he did not share his neighbours' love of sport of any description, nor did he care for society, and because of all this he was regarded as peculiar, not to say eccentric. But he was deeply interested in agriculture, especially in cattle and their improvement, and that object grew to be his master passion. It was a period of great depression, and as his farms fell vacant he took them into his own hands, increased his stock and built model cowhouses, and came at last to be known throughout his own country, and eventually everywhere, as one of the biggest cattle-breeders in England. But he was famous in a peculiar way. Wise breeders and buyers shook their heads and even touched their foreheads significantly, and predicted that the squire of Norton would finish by ruining himself. They were right, he ruined himself; not that he was mentally weaker than those who watched and cunningly exploited him; he was ruined because his object was a higher one than theirs. He saw clearly that the prize system is a vicious one and that better results may be obtained without it. He proved this at a heavy cost by breeding better beasts than his rivals, who were all exhibitors and prizewinners, and who by this means got their advertisements and secured the highest prices, while he, who disdained prizes and looked with disgust at the overfed and polished animals at shows, got no advertisements and was compelled to sell at unremunerative prices. The buyers, it may be mentioned, were always the breeders for shows, and they made a splendid profit out of it.

He carried on the fight for a good many years, becoming more and more involved, until his creditors took possession of the estate, sold off the stock, let the farms, and succeeded in finding a tenant for the furnished house. He went to a cottage in the village and there passed his remaining years. To the world he appeared unmoved by his reverses. The change from mansion and park to a small thatched cottage, with a labourer's wife for attendant, made no change in the man, nor did he resign his seat on the Bench of Magistrates or any other unpaid office he held. To the last he was what he had always been, formal and ceremonious, more gracious to those beneath him than to equals; strict in the performance of his duties, living with extreme frugality and giving freely to those in want, and very regular in his attendance at church, where he would sit facing the tombs and memorials of his ancestors, among the people but not of them – a man alone and apart, respected by all but loved by none.

Finally he died and was buried with the others, and one more memorial with the old name, which he bore last, was placed on the wall. That was the story as it was told me, and as it was all about a man who was without charm and had no love interest it did not greatly interest me, and I soon dismissed it from my thoughts. Then one day coming through a grove in the park and finding myself standing before the ancient, empty, desolate house – for on the squire's death everything had been sold and taken away – I remembered that the caretaker had begged me to let him show me over the place. I had not felt inclined to gratify him, as I had found him a young man of a too active mind whose only desire was to capture some person to talk to and unfold his original ideas and schemes, but now having come to the house I thought I would suffer him, and soon found him at work in the vast old walled garden. He joyfully threw down his spade and let me in and then up to the top floor, determined that I should see everything. By the time we got down to the ground floor I was pretty tired of empty rooms, oak panelled, and passages and oak staircases, and of talk, and impatient to get away. But no, I had not seen the housekeeper's room – I must see that! – and so into another great vacant room I was dragged, and to keep me as long as possible in that last room he began unlocking and flinging open all the old oak cupboards and presses. Glancing round at the long array of empty shelves, I noticed a small brown-paper parcel, thick with dust, in a corner, and as it was the only movable thing I had seen in that vacant house I asked him what the parcel contained. Books, he replied – they had been left as of no value when the house was cleared of furniture. As I wished to see the books he undid the parcel; it contained forty copies of a small quarto-shaped book of sonnets, with the late squire's name as author on the title page. I read a sonnet, and told him I should like to read them all. 'You can have a copy, of course,' he exclaimed. 'Put it in your pocket and keep it.' When I asked him if he had any right to give one away he laughed and said that if any one had thought the whole parcel worth two-pence it would not have been left behind. He was quite right; a cracked dinner – plate or a saucepan with a hole in it or an earthenware teapot with a broken spout would not have been left, but the line was drawn at a book of sonnets by the late squire. Nobody wanted it, and so without more qualms I put it in my pocket, and have it before me now, opened at page 63, on which appears, without a headline, the sonnet I first read, and which I quote:

> How beautiful are birds, of God's sweet air
>   Free denizens; no ugly earthly spot
>   Their boundless happiness doth seem to blot.
> The swallow, swiftly flying here and there,
> Can it be true that dreary household care
>   Doth goad her to incessant flight? If not
>   How can it be that she doth cast her lot
> Now there, now here, pursuing summer everywhere?
>   I sadly fear that shallow, tiny brain
> Is not exempt from anxious cares and fears,
>   That mingled heritage of joy and pain
> That for some reason everywhere appears;
>   And yet those birds, how beautiful they are!
>   Sure beauty is to happiness no bar.

This has a fault that *doth* offend the reader of modern verse, and there are many of the eighty sonnets in the book which do not equal it in merit. He was manifestly an amateur; he sometimes writes with labour, and he not infrequently ends with the unpardonable weak line. Nevertheless he had rightly chosen this difficult form in which to express his inner self. It suited his grave, concentrated thought, and each little imperfect poem of fourteen lines gives us a glimpse into a wise, beneficent mind. He had fought his fight and suffered defeat, and had then withdrawn himself silently from the field to die. But if he had been embittered he could have relieved himself in this little book. There is no trace of such a feeling. He only asks, in one sonnet, where can a balm be found for the heart fretted and torn with eternal cares; when we have thought and striven for some great and good purpose, when all our striving has ended in disaster? *His* plan, he concludes, is to go out in the quiet night-time and look at the stars.

Here let me quote two more sonnets written in contemplative mood, just to give the reader a fuller idea not of the verse, as verse, but of the spirit in the old squire. There is no title to these two:

I like a fire of wood; there is a kind
   Of artless poetry in all its ways:
   When first 'tis lighted, how it roars and plays,
And sways to every breath its flames, refined
By fancy to some shape by life confined.
   And then how touching are its latter days;
   When, all its strength decayed, and spent the blaze
Of fiery youth, grey ash is all we find.
   Perhaps we know the tree, of which the pile
Once formed a part, and oft beneath its shade
     Have sported in our youth; or in quaint style
       Have carved upon its rugged bark a name
       Of which the memory doth alone remain –
A memory doomed, alas! in turn to fade.

Bad enough as verse, the critic will say; refined, confined, find – what poor rhymes are these! and he will think me wrong to draw these frailties from their forgotten abode. But I like to think of the solitary old man sitting by his wood fire in the old house, not brooding bitterly on his frustrate life, but putting his quiet thoughts into the form of a sonnet. The other is equally good – or bad, if the critic will have it so:

The clock had just struck five, and all was still
   Within my house, when straight I open threw
   With eager hand the casement dim with dew.
Oh, what a glorious flush of light did fill
That old staircase! and then and there did kill
   All those black doubts that ever do renew
   Their civil war with all that's good and true
Within our hearts, when body and mind are ill
   From this slight incident I would infer
   A cheerful truth, that men without demur,
In times of stress and doubt, throw open wide
The windows of their breast; nor stung by pride
   In stifling darkness gloomily abide;
   But bid the light flow in on either side.

A 'slight incident' and a beautiful thought. But all I have so far said about the little book is preliminary to what I wish to say about another

sonnet which must also be quoted. It is perhaps, as a sonnet, as ill done
as the others, but the subject of it specially attracted me, as it happened to be one which was much in my mind during my week's stay at
Norton.

That remote little village without a squire or any person of means
or education in or near it capable of feeling the slightest interest in
the people, except the parson, an old infirm man who was never seen
but once a week – how wanting in some essential thing it appeared! It
seemed to me that the one thing which might be done in these small
centres of rural life to brighten and beautify existence is precisely the
thing which is never done, also that what really is being done is of
doubtful value and sometimes actually harmful.

Leaving Norton one day I visited other small villages in the neighbourhood and found they were no better off. I had heard of the rector
of one of these villages as a rather original man, and went and discussed
the subject with him. 'It is quite useless thinking about it,' he said. 'The
people here are clods, and will not respond to any effort you can make
to introduce a little light and sweetness into their lives.' There was no
more to be said to him, but I knew he was wrong. I found the villagers
in that part of the country the most intelligent and responsive people of
their class I had ever encountered. It was a delightful experience to go
into their cottages, not to read them a homily or to present them with a
book or a shilling, nor to inquire into their welfare, material and spiritual, but to converse intimately with a human interest in them, as would
be the case in a country where there are no caste distinctions. It was
delightful, because they were so responsive, so sympathetic, so alive.

Now it was just at this time, when the subject was in my mind, that
the book of sonnets came into my hands – given to me by the generous
caretaker – and I read in it this one on 'Innocent Amusements':

> There lacks a something to complete the round
>   Of our fair England's homely happiness -
>   A something, yet how oft do trifles bless
> When greater gifts by far redound
> To honours lone, but no responsive sound
>   Of joy or mirth awake, nay, oft oppress,
>   While gifts of which we scarce the moment guess
> In never-failing joys abound.

No nation can be truly great
    That hath not something childlike in its life
        Of every day; it should its youth renew
With simple joys that sweetly recreate
    The jaded mind, conjoined in friendly strife
        The pleasures of its childhood's days pursue.

What wise and kindly thoughts he had – the old squire of Norton!
Surely, when telling me the story of his life, they had omitted something!
I questioned them on the point. Did he not in all the years he was at
Norton House, and later when he lived among them in a cottage in the
village – did he not go into their homes and meet them as if he knew
and felt that they were all of the same flesh, children of one universal
Father, and did he not make them feel this about him – that the differences in fortune and position and education were mere accidents? And
the answer was: No, certainly not! as if I had asked a preposterous
question. He was the squire, a gentleman – any one might understand
that he could not come among them like that! That is what a parson can
do because he is, so to speak, paid to keep an eye on them, and besides
it's religion there and a different thing. But the squire! – *their* squire,
that dignified old gentleman, so upright in his saddle, so considerate
and courteous to everyone – but he never forgot his position – never in
that way! I also asked if he had never tried to establish, or advocated,
or suggested to them any kind of reunions to take place from time to
time, or an entertainment or festival to get them to come pleasantly
together, making a brightness in their lives – something which would
not be cricket or football, nor any form of sport for a few of the men,
all the others being mere lookers-on and the women and children left
out altogether; something which would be for and include everyone,
from the oldest grey labourer no longer able to work to the toddling
little ones; something of their own invention, peculiar to Norton, which
would be their pride and make their village dearer to them? And the
answer was still no, and no, and no. He had never attempted, never
suggested, anything of the sort. How could he – the squire! Yet he wrote
those wise words:

No nation can be truly great
    That hath not something childlike in its life
        Of every day.

Why are we lacking in that which others undoubtedly have, a something to complete the round of homely happiness in our little rural centres; how is it that we do not properly encourage the things which, albeit childlike, are essential, which sweetly recreate? It is not merely the selfishness of those who are well placed and prefer to live for themselves, or who have light but care not to shed it on those who are not of their class. Selfishness is common enough everywhere, in men of all races. It is not selfishness, nor the growth of towns or decay of agriculture, which as a fact does not decay, nor education, nor any of the other causes usually given for the dullness, the greyness of village life. The chief cause, I take it, is that gulf, or barrier, which exists between men and men in different classes in our country, or a considerable portion of it – the caste feeling which is becoming increasingly rigid in the rural world, if my own observation, extending over a period of twenty-five years, is not all wrong.

CHAPTER ELEVEN

Salisbury and its Doves

Never in my experience has there been a worse spring season than that of 1903 for the birds, more especially for the short-winged migrants. In April I looked for the woodland warblers and found them not, or saw but a few of the commonest kinds. It was only too easy to account for this rarity. The bitter north-east wind had blown every day and all day long during those weeks when birds are coming, and when nearing the end of their journey, at its most perilous stage, the wind had been dead against them; its coldness and force was too much for these delicate travellers, and doubtless they were beaten down in thousands into the grey waters of a bitter sea. The stronger-winged wheatear was more fortunate, since he comes in March, and before that spell of deadly weather he was already back in his breeding haunts on Salisbury Plain, and, in fact, everywhere on that open down country. I was there to hear him sing his wild notes to the listening waste – singing them, as his pretty fashion is, up in the air, suspended on quickly vibrating wings like a great black and white moth. But he was in no singing mood, and at last, in desperation, I fled to Salisbury to wait for loitering spring in that unattractive town.

The streets were cold as the open plain, and there was no comfort indoors; to haunt the cathedral during those vacant days was the only occupation left to me. There was some shelter to be had under the walls, and the empty, vast interior would seem almost cosy on coming in from the wind. At service my due feet never failed, while morning, noon, and evening I paced the smooth level green by the hour, standing at intervals to gaze up at the immense pile with its central soaring spire, asking myself why I had never greatly liked it in the past and did not like it much better now when grown familiar with it. Undoubtedly it is one of the noblest structures of its kind in England – even my eyes that look coldly on most buildings could see it; and I could admire, even reverence, but could not love. It suffers by comparison with other temples into which my soul has wandered. It has not the majesty and appearance of immemorial age, the dim religious richness of the interior, with much else that goes to make up, without and within, the *expression* which is so marked in other mediaeval fanes – Winchester, Ely, York,

Canterbury, Exeter, and Wells. To the dry, mechanical mind of the architect these great cathedrals are in the highest degree imperfect, according to the rules of his art: to all others this imperfectness is their chief excellence and glory; for they are in a sense a growth, a flower of many minds and many periods, and are imperfect even as Nature is, in her rocks and trees; and, being in harmony with Nature and like Nature, they are inexpressibly beautiful and satisfying beyond all buildings to the aesthetic as well as to the religious sense.

Occasionally I met and talked with an old man employed at the cathedral. One day, closing one eye and shading the other with his hand, he gazed up at the building for some time, and then remarked: 'I'll tell you what's wrong with Salisbury – it looks too noo.' He was near the mark; the fault is that to the professional eye it is faultless; the lack of expression is due to the fact that it came complete from its maker's brain, like a coin from the mint, and being all on one symmetrical plan it has the trim, neat appearance of a toy cathedral carved out of wood and set on a green-painted square.

After all, my thoughts and criticisms on the cathedral, as a building, were merely incidental; my serious business was with the feathered people to be seen there. Few in the woods and fewer on the windy downs, here birds were abundant, not only on the building, where they were like seafowl congregated on a precipitous rock, but they were all about me. The level green was the hunting ground of many thrushes – a dozen or twenty could often be seen at one time – and it was easy to spot those that had young. The worm they dragged out was not devoured; another was looked for, then another; then all were cut up in proper lengths and beaten and bruised, and finally packed into a bundle and carried off. Rooks, too, were there, breeding on the cathedral elms, and had no time and spirit to wrangle, but could only caw-caw distressfully at the wind, which tossed them hither and thither in the air and lashed the tall trees, threatening at each fresh gust to blow their nests to pieces. Small birds of half a dozen kinds were also there, and one tinkle-tinkled his spring song quite merrily in spite of the cold that kept the others silent and made me blue. One day I spied a big queen bumble-bee on the ground, looking extremely conspicuous in its black and chestnut coat on the fresh green sward; and thinking it numbed by the cold I picked it up. It moved its legs feebly, but alas! its enemy had found and struck it down, and with its hard, sharp little beak had drilled a hole in one of the upper plates of its abdomen, and from that small opening had cunningly extracted all the meat. Though still alive it was empty as a blown eggshell. Poor queen and mother, you survived the winter in vain, and went abroad in vain in the bitter weather in quest of bread to nourish your few first-born – the grubs that would help you by and by; now there will be no bread for them, and for you no populous city in the flowery earth and a great crowd of children to rise up each day, when days are long, to call you blessed! And he who did this thing, the unspeakable oxeye with his black and yellow breast – 'satanic black and amber' – even while I made my lamentation was tinkling his merry song overhead in the windy elms.

The birds that lived on the huge cathedral itself had the greatest attraction for me; and here the daws, if not the most numerous, were the most noticeable, as they ever are on account of their conspicuousness in their black plumage, their loquacity and everlasting restlessness. Far up on the ledge from which the spire rises a kestrel had found a cosy corner in which to establish himself, and one day when I was there a number of daws took it on themselves to eject him: they gathered near and flew this way and that, and cawed and cawed in anger, and swooped at him, until he could stand their insults no longer, and, suddenly dashing out, he struck and buffeted them right and left and sent them screaming with fear in all directions. After this they left him in peace: they had forgotten that he was a hawk, and that even the gentle mousing wind-hover has a nobler spirit than any crow of them all.

On first coming to the cathedral I noticed a few pigeons sitting on the roof and ledges very high up, and, not seeing them well, I assumed that they were of the common or domestic kind. By and by one cooed, then another; and recognizing the stock-dove note I began to look carefully, and found that all the birds on the building – about thirty pairs – were of this species. It was a great surprise, for though we occasionally find a pair of stock-doves breeding on the ivied wall of some inhabited mansion in the country, it was a new thing to find a considerable colony of this shy woodland species established on a building in a town. They lived and bred there just as the common pigeon – the vari-coloured descendant of the blue rock – does on St. Paul's, the Law Courts, and the British Museum in London. Only, unlike our metropolitan doves, both the domestic kind and the ringdove in the parks, the Salisbury doves though in the town are not of it. They come not down to mix with the currents of human life in the streets and open spaces; they fly away to the country to feed, and dwell on the cathedral above the houses and people just as sea-birds – kittiwake and guillemot and gannet – dwell on the ledges of some vast ocean-fronting cliff.

The old man mentioned above told me that the birds were called 'rocks' by the townspeople, also that they had been there for as long as he could remember. Six or seven years ago, he said, when the repairs to the roof and spire were started, the pigeons began to go away until there was not one left. The work lasted three years, and immediately on its conclusion the doves began to return, and were now as numerous as formerly. How, I inquired, did these innocent birds get on with their black neighbours, seeing that the daw is a cunning creature much given to persecution – a crow, in fact, as black as any of his family? They got on badly, he said; the doves were early breeders, beginning in March, and were allowed to have the use of the holes until the daws wanted them at the end of April, when they forcibly ejected the young doves. He said that in spring he always picked up a good many young doves, often unfledged, thrown down by the daws. I did not doubt his story. I had just found a young bird myself – a little blue-skinned, yellow-mouthed fledgling which had fallen sixty or seventy feet on to the gravel below. But in June, he said, when the daws brought off their young, the doves entered into possession once more, and were then permitted to rear their young in peace.

I returned to Salisbury about the middle of May in better weather, when there were days that were almost genial, and found the cathedral a greater 'habitacle of birds' than ever: starlings, swifts, and swallows were there, the lively little martins in hundreds, and the doves and daws in their usual numbers. All appeared to be breeding, and for some time I saw no quarreling. At length I spied a pair of doves with a nest in a small cavity in the stone at the back of a narrow ledge about seventy feet from the ground, and by standing back some distance I could see the hen bird sitting on the nest, while the cock stood outside on the ledge keeping guard. I watched this pair for some hours and saw a jackdaw sweep down on them a dozen or more times at long intervals. Sometimes after swooping down he would alight on the ledge a yard or two away, and the male dove would then turn and face him, and if he then began sidling up the dove would dash at and buffet him with his wings with the greatest violence and throw him off. When he swooped closer the dove would spring up and meet him in the air, striking him at the moment of meeting, and again the daw would be beaten. When I left three days after witnessing this contest, the doves were still in possession of their nest, and I concluded that they were not so entirely at the mercy of the jackdaw as the old man had led me to believe.

It was, on this occasion, a great pleasure to listen to the doves. The stock-dove has no set song, like the ringdove, but like all the other species in the typical genus *Columba* it has the cooing or family note, one of the most human-like sounds which birds emit. In the stock-dove this is a better, more musical, and a more varied sound than in any other Columba known to me. The pleasing quality of the sound as well as the variety in it could be well noted here where the birds were many, scattered about on ledges and projections high above the earth, and when bird after bird uttered its plaint, each repeating his note half a dozen to a dozen times, one in slow measured time, and deep-voiced like the rock-dove, but more musical; another rapidly, with shorter, impetuous notes in a higher key, as if carried away by excitement. There were not two birds that cooed in precisely the same way, and the same bird would often vary its manner of cooing.

It was best to hear them during the afternoon service in the cathedral, when the singing of the choir and throbbing and pealing of the organ which filled the vast interior was heard outside, subdued by the walls through which it passed, and was like a beautiful mist or atmosphere of sound pervading and enveloping the great building; and when the plaining of the doves, owing to the rhythmic flow of the notes and their human characters, seemed to harmonize with and be a part of that sacred music.

CHAPTER TWELVE

Whitesheet Hill

On Easter Saturday the roadsides and copses by the little river Nadder were full of children gathering primroses; they might have filled a thousand baskets without the flowers being missed, so abundant were they in that place. Cold though it was the whole air was laden with the delicious fragrance. It was pleasant to see and talk with the little people occupied with the task they loved so well, and I made up my mind to see the result of all this flower-gathering next day in some of the village churches in the neighbourhood – Fovant, Teffont Evias, Chilmark, Swallowcliffe, Tisbury, and Fonthill Bishop. I had counted on some improvement in the weather – some bright sunshine to light up the flower-decorated interiors; but Easter Sunday proved colder than ever, with the bitter north-east still blowing, the grey travelling cloud still covering the sky; and so to get the full benefit of the bitterness I went instead to spend my day on the top of the biggest down above the valley. That was Whitesheet Hill, and forms the highest part of the long ridge dividing the valleys of the Ebble and Nadder.

It was roughest and coldest up there, and suited my temper best, for when the weather seems spiteful one finds a grim sort of satisfaction in defying it. On a genial day it would have been very pleasant on that lofty plain, for the flat top of the vast down is like a plain in appearance, and the earthworks on it show that it was once a populous habitation of man. Now because of the wind and cloud its aspect was bare and bleak and desolate, and after roaming about for an hour, exploring the thickest furze patches, I began to think that my day would have to be spent in solitude, without a living creature to keep me company. The birds had apparently all been blown away and the rabbits were staying at home in their burrows. Not even an insect could I see, although the furze was in full blossom; the honey-suckers were out of sight and torpid, and the bloom itself could no longer look 'unprofitably gay,' as the poet says it does. 'Not even a wheatear!' I said, for I had counted on that bird in the intervals between the storms, although I knew I should not hear his wild delightful warble in such weather.

Then, all at once, I beheld that very bird, a solitary female, flittering on over the flat ground before me, perching on the little green ant-mounds and flirting its tail and bobbing as if greatly excited at my presence in that lonely place. I wondered where its mate was, following it from place to place as it flew, determined now I had found a bird to keep it in sight. Presently a great blackness appeared low down in the cloudy sky, and rose and spread, travelling fast towards me, and the little wheatear fled in fear from it and vanished from sight over the rim of the down. But I was there to defy the weather, and so instead of following the bird in search of shelter I sat down among some low furze bushes and waited and watched. By and by I caught sight of three magpies, rising one by one at long intervals from the furze and flying laboriously towards a distant hill-top grove of pines. Then I heard the wailing cry of a peewit, and caught sight of the bird at a distance, and soon afterwards a sound of another character – the harsh angry cry of a carrion crow, almost as deep as the raven's angry voice. Before long I discovered the bird at a great height coming towards me in hot pursuit of a kestrel. They passed directly over me so that I had them a long time in sight, the kestrel travelling quietly on in the face of the wind, the crow toiling after, and at intervals spurting till he got near enough to hurl himself at his enemy, emitting his croaks of rage. For invariably the kestrel with one of his sudden swallow-like turns avoided the blow and went on as before. I watched them until they were lost to sight in the coming blackness and wondered that so intelligent a creature as a crow should waste his energies in that vain chase. Still one could understand it and even sympathize with him. For the kestrel is a most insulting creature towards the bigger birds. He knows that they are incapable of paying him out, and when he finds them off their guard he will drop down and inflict a blow just for the fun of the thing. This outraged crow appeared determined to have his revenge.

Then the storm broke on me, and so fiercely did the rain and sleet thrash me that, fearing a cold soaking, I fled before it to the rim of the plain, where the wheatear had vanished, and saw a couple of hundred yards down on the smooth steep slope a thicket of dwarf trees. It was, the only shelter in sight, and to it I went, to discover much to my disgust that the trees were nothing but elders. For there is no tree that affords so poor a shelter, especially on the high open downs, where the foliage is scantier than in other situations and lets in the wind and rain in full force upon you.

But the elder affects me in two ways. I like it on account of early associations, and because the birds delight in its fruit, though they wisely refuse to build in its branches; and I dislike it because its smell is offensive to me and its berries the least pleasant of all wild fruits to my taste. I can eat ivy-berries in March, and yew in its season, poison or not; and hips and haws and holly-berries and harsh acorn, and the rowan, which some think acrid; but the elderberry I can't stomach.

How comes it, I have asked more than once, that this poor tree is so often seen on the downs where it is so badly fitted to be and makes so sorry an appearance with its weak branches broken and its soft leaves torn by the winds? How badly it contrasts with the other trees and bushes that flourish on the downs – furze, juniper, holly, blackthorn, and hawthorn!

Two years ago, one day in the early spring, I was walking on an extensive down in another part of Wiltshire with the tenant of the land, who began there as a large sheep-farmer, but eventually finding that he could make more with rabbits than with sheep turned most of his land into a warren. The higher part of this down was overgrown with furze, mixed with holly and other bushes, but the slopes were mostly very bare. At one spot on a wide bare slope where the rabbits had formed a big group of burrows there was a close little thicket of young elder trees, looking exceedingly conspicuous in the bright green of early April. Calling my companion's attention to this little thicket I said something about the elder growing on the open downs where it always appeared to be out of harmony with its surroundings. 'I don't suppose you planted elders here,' I said.

'No, but I know who did,' he returned, and he then gave me this curious history of the trees. Five years before, the rabbits, finding it a suitable spot to dig in, probably because of a softer chalk there, made a number of deep burrows at that spot. When the wheatears, or 'horse-maggers' as he called them, returned in spring two or three pairs attached themselves to this group of burrows and bred in them. There was that season a solitary elder-bush higher up on the down among the furze which bore a heavy crop of berries; and when the fruit was ripe he watched the birds feeding on it, the wheatears among them. The following spring seedlings came up out of the loose earth heaped about the rabbit burrows, and as they were not cut down by the rabbits, for they dislike the elder, they grew up, and now formed a clump of fifty or sixty little trees of six feet to eight feet in height.

Who would have thought to find a tree-planter in the wheatear, the bird of the stony waste and open naked down, who does not even ask for a bush to perch on?

It then occurred to me that in every case where I had observed a clump of elder bushes on the bare downside, it grew upon a village or collection of rabbit burrows, and it is probable that in every case the clump owed its existence to the wheatears who had dropped the seed about their nesting-place.

The clump where I had sought a shelter from the storm was composed of large old dilapidated-looking half-dead elders; perhaps their age was not above thirty or forty years, but they looked older than hawthorns of one or two centuries; and under them the rabbits had their diggings – huge old mounds and burrows that looked like a badger's earth. Here, too, the burrows had probably existed first and had attracted the wheatears, and the birds had brought the seed from some distant bush.

Crouching down in one of the big burrows at the roots of an old elder I remained for half an hour, listening to the thump-thump of the alarmed rabbits about me, and the accompanying hiss and swish of the wind and sleet and rain in the ragged branches.

The storm over I continued my rambles on Whitesheet Hill, and coming back an hour or two later to the very spot where I had seen and followed the wheatear, I all at once caught sight of a second bird, lying dead on the turf close to my feet! The sudden sight gave me a shock of astonishment, mingled with admiration and grief. For how pretty it looked, though dead, lying on its back, the little black legs stuck stiffly up, the long wings pressed against the sides, their black tips touching together like the clasped hands of a corpse; and the fan-like black and white tail, half open as in life, moved perpetually up and down by the wind, as if that tail-flirting action of the bird had continued after death. It was very beautiful in its delicate shape and pale harmonious colouring, resting on the golden-green mossy turf. And it was a male, undoubtedly the mate of the wheatear I had seen at the spot, and its little mate, not knowing what death is, had probably been keeping watch near it, wondering at its strange stillness and greatly fearing for its safety when I came that way, and passed by without seeing it.

Poor little migrant, did you come back across half the world for this – back to your home on Whitesheet Hill to grow cold and fail in the cold April wind, and finally to look very pretty, lying stiff and cold, to the one pair of human eyes that were destined to see you! The little birds that come and go and return to us over such vast distances, they perish like this in myriads annually; flying to and from us they are blown away by death like sere autumn leaves, 'the pestilence-stricken multitudes' whirled away by the wind! They die in myriads: that is not strange; the strange, the astonishing thing is the fact of death; what can they tell us of it – the wise men who live or have ever lived on the earth – what can they say now of the bright intelligent spirit, the dear little emotional soul, that had so fit a tenement and so fitly expressed itself in motions of such exquisite grace, in melody so sweet! Did it go out like the glow-worm's lamp, the life and sweetness of the flower? Was its destiny not like that of the soul, specialized in a different direction, of the saint or poet or philosopher! Alas, they can tell us nothing!

I could not go away leaving it in that exposed place on the turf, to be found a little later by a magpie or carrion crow or fox, and devoured. Close by there was a small round hillock, an old forsaken nest of the little brown ants, green and soft with moss and small creeping herbs – a suitable grave for a wheatear. Cutting out a round piece of turf from the side, I made a hole with my stick and put the dead bird in and replacing the turf left it neatly buried.

It was not that I had or have any quarrel with the creatures I have named, or would have them other than they are – carrion-eaters and scavengers, Nature's balance-keepers and purifiers. The only creatures on earth I loathe and hate are the gourmets, the carrion-crows and foxes of the human kind who devour wheatears and skylarks at their tables.

CHAPTER THIRTEEN

Bath and Wells Revisited

'Tis so easy to get from London to Bath, by merely stepping into a railway carriage which takes you smoothly without a stop in two short hours from Paddington, that I was amazed at myself in having allowed five full years to pass since my previous visit. The question was much in my mind as I strolled about noting the old-remembered names of streets and squares and crescents. Quiet Street was the name inscribed on one; it was, to me, the secret name of them all. The old impressions were renewed, an old feeling partially recovered. The wide, clean ways; the solid, stone-built houses with their dignified aspect; the large distances, terrace beyond terrace; mansions and vast green lawns and parks and gardens; avenues and groups of stately trees, especially that unmatched clump of old planes in the Circus; the whole town, the design in the classic style of one master mind, set by the Avon, amid green hills, produced a sense of harmony and repose which cannot be equalled by any other town in the kingdom.

This idle time was delightful so long as I gave my attention exclusively to houses from the outside, and to hills, rocks, trees, waters, and all visible nature, which here harmonizes with man's works. To sit on some high hill and look down on Bath, sun-flushed or half veiled in mist; to lounge on Camden Crescent, or climb Sion Hill, or take my ease with the water-drinkers in the spacious, comfortable Pump Room; or, better still, to rest at noon in the ancient abbey – all this was pleasure pure and simple, a quiet drifting back until I found myself younger by five years than I had taken myself to be.

I haunted the abbey, and the more I saw of it the more I loved it. The impression it had made on me during my former visits had faded, or else I had never properly seen it, or had not seen it in the right emotional mood. Now I began to think it the best of all the great abbey churches of England and the equal of the cathedrals in its effect on the mind. How rich the interior is in its atmosphere of tempered light or tender gloom! How tall and graceful the columns holding up the high roof of white stone with its marvellous palm-leaf sculpture! What a vast expanse of beautifully stained glass! I certainly gave myself plenty of time to appreciate it on this occasion, as I visited it every day, sometimes two or three times, and not infrequently I sat there for an hour at a stretch.

Sitting there one day, thinking of nothing, I was gradually awakened to a feeling almost of astonishment at the sight of the extraordinary number of memorial tablets of every imaginable shape and size which crowd the walls. So numerous are they and so closely placed that you could not find space anywhere to put your hand against the wall. We are accustomed to think that in cathedrals and other great ecclesiastical buildings the illustrious dead receive burial, and their names and claims on our gratitude and reverence are recorded, but in no fane in the land is there so numerous a gathering of the dead as in this place. The inscription-covered walls were like the pages of an old black-letter volume without margins. Yet when I came to think of it I could not recall any Bath celebrity or great person associated with Bath except Beau Nash, who was not perhaps a very great person. Probably Carlyle would have described him as a 'meeserable creature.'

Leaving my seat I began to examine the inscriptions, and found that they had not been placed there in memory of men belonging to Bath or even Somerset. These monuments were erected to persons from all counties in the three kingdoms, and from all the big towns, those to Londoners being most numerous. Nor were they of persons distinguished in any way. Here you find John or Henry or Thomas Smith, or Brown, or Jones, or Robinson, provision dealer, or merchant, of Clerkenwell, or Bermondsey, or Bishopsgate Street Within or Without; also many retired captains, majors, and colonels. There were hundreds more whose professions or occupations in life were not stated. There were also hundreds of memorials to ladies – widows and spinsters. They were all, in fact, to persons who had come to die in Bath after 'taking the waters,' and dying, they or their friends had purchased immortality on the walls of the abbey with a handful or two of gold. Here is one of several inscriptions of the kind I took the trouble to copy: 'His early virtues, his cultivated talents, his serious piety, inexpressibly endeared him to his friends and opened to them many bright prospects of excellence and happiness. These prospects have all faded,' and so on for several long lines in very big letters, occupying a good deal of space on the wall. But what and who was he, and what connection had he with Bath? He was a young man born in the West Indies who died in Scotland, and later his mother, coming to Bath for her health, 'caused this inscription to be placed on the abbey walls'!

If this policy or tradition is still followed by the abbey authorities, it will be necessary for them to build an annexe; if it be no longer followed, would it be going too far to suggest that these mural tablets to a thousand obscurities, which ought never to have been placed there, should now be removed and placed in some vault where the relations or descendants of the persons described could find, and if they wished it, have them removed?

But it must be said that the abbey is not without a fair number of memorials with which no one can quarrel; the one I admire most, to Quin, the actor, has, I think, the best or the most appropriate epitaph ever written. No, one, however familiar with the words, will find fault with me for quoting them here:

> That tongue which set the table on a roar
> And charmed the public ear is heard no more.
> Closed are those eyes, the harbingers of wit,
> Which spake before the tongue what Shakespeare writ.
> Cold is that hand which living was stretched forth
> At friendship's call to succor modest worth.
> Here lies James Quin; deign, readers, to be taught,
> Whate'er thy strength of body, force of thought,
> In Nature's happiest mood however cast,
> To this complexion thou must come at last.

Quin's monument strikes one as the greatest there because of Garrick's living words, but there is another very much more beautiful.

I first noticed this memorial on the wall at a distance of about three yards, too far to read anything in the inscription except the name of Sibthorpe, which was strange to me, but instead of going nearer to read it I remained standing to admire it at that distance. The tablet was of white marble, and on it was sculptured the figure of a young man with curly head and classic profile. He was wearing sandals and a loose mantle held to his breast with one hand, while in the other hand he carried a bunch of leaves and flowers. He appeared in the act of stepping ashore from a boat of antique shape, and the artist had been singularly successful in producing the idea of free and vigorous motion in the figure as well as of some absorbing object in his mind. The figure was undoubtedly symbolical, and I began to amuse myself by trying to guess its meaning. Then a curious thing happened. A person who had been

moving slowly along near me, apparently looking with no great interest at the memorials, came past me and glanced first at the tablet I was
looking at, then at me. As our eyes met I remarked that I was admiring
the best memorial I had found in the abbey, and then added, 'I've been
trying to make out its meaning. You see the man is a traveller and is
stepping ashore with a flowering spray in his hand. It strikes me that it
may have been erected to the memory of a person who introduced some
valuable plant into England.'

'Yes, perhaps,' he said. 'But who was he?'

'I don't know yet,' I returned. 'I can only see that his name was
Sibthorpe.'

'Sibthorpe!' he exclaimed excitedly. 'Why, this is the very memorial
I've been looking for all over the abbey and had pretty well given up
all hopes of finding it.' With that he went to it and began studying
the inscription, which was in Latin. John Sibthorpe, I found, was a
distinguished botanist, author of the *Flora Graeca*, who died over a
century ago.

I asked him why he was interested in Sibthorpe's memorial.

'Well, you see, I'm a great botanist myself,' he explained, 'and have
been familiar with his name and work all my life. Of course,' he added,
'I don't mean I'm great in the sense that Sibthorpe was. I'm only a little
local botanist, quite unknown outside my own circle; I only mean that
I'm a great lover of botany.'

I left him there, and had the curiosity to look up the great man's life,
and found some very curious things in it. He was a son of Humphrey
Sibthorpe, also a great botanist, who succeeded the still greater Dille-
nius as Sherardian Professor of Botany at Oxford, a post which he held
for thirty-six years, and during that time he delivered one lecture, which
was a failure. John, if he did not suck in botany with his mother's milk,
took it quite early from his father, and on leaving the University went
abroad to continue his studies. Eventually he went to Greece, inflamed
with the ambition to identify all the plants mentioned by Dioscorides.
Then he set about writing his *Flora Graeca*; but he had a rough time
of it travelling about in that rude land, and falling ill he had to leave
his work undone. When nearing his end he came to Bath, like so many
other afflicted ones, only to die, and he was very properly buried in
the abbey. In his will he left an estate the proceeds of which were to
be devoted to the completion of his work, which was to be in ten folio

volumes, with one hundred plates in each. This was done and the work finished forty-four years after his death, when thirty copies were issued to the patient subscribers at two hundred and forty guineas a copy. But the whole cost of the work was set down at 30,000 pounds! A costlier work it would be hard to find; I wonder how many of us have seen it?

But I must go back to my subject. I was not in Bath just to die and lie there, like poor Sibthorpe, with all those strange bedfellows of his, nor was I in search of a vacant space the size of my hand on the walls to bespeak it for my own memorial. On the contrary, I was there, as we have seen, to knock five years off my age. And it was very pleasant, as I have said, so long as I confined my attention to Bath, the stone-built town of old memories and associations – so long as I was satisfied to loiter in the streets and wide green places and in the Pump Room and the abbey. The bitter came in only when, going from places to faces, I began to seek out the friends and acquaintances of former days. The familiar faces seemed not wholly familiar now. A change had been wrought; in some cases a great change, as in that of some weedy girl who had blossomed into fair womanhood. One could not grieve at that; but in the middle-aged and those who were verging on or past that period, it was impossible not to feel saddened at the difference. 'I see no change in you,' is a lie ready to the lips which would speak some pleasing thing, but it does not quite convince. Men are naturally brutal, and use no compliments to one another; on the contrary, they do not hesitate to make a joke of wrinkles and grey hairs – their own and yours. 'But, oh, the difference' when the familiar face, no longer familiar as of old, is a woman's! This is no light thing to her, and her eyes, being preternaturally keen in such matters, see not only the change in you, but what is infinitely sadder, the changed reflection of herself. Your eyes have revealed the shock you have experienced. You cannot hide it; her heart is stabbed with a sudden pain, and she is filled with shame and confusion; and the pain is but greater if her life has glided smoothly – if she cannot appeal to your compassion, finding a melancholy relief in that saddest cry:

O Grief has changed me since you saw me last!

For not grief, nor sickness, nor want, nor care, nor any misery or calamity which men fear, is her chief enemy. Time alone she hates and fears – insidious Time who has lulled her mind with pleasant flatteries all these years while subtly taking away her most valued possessions, the bloom and colour, the grace, the sparkle, the charm of other years.

Here is a true and pretty little story, which may or may not exactly fit the theme, but is very well worth telling. A lady of fashion, middle-aged or thereabouts, good-looking but pale and with the marks of care and disillusionment on her expressive face, accompanied by her pretty sixteen-years-old daughter, one day called on an artist and asked him to show her his studio. He was a very great artist, the greatest portrait-painter we have ever had and he did not know who she was, but with the sweet courtesy which distinguished him through all his long life – he died recently at a very advanced age – he at once put his work away and took her round his studio to show her everything he thought would interest her. But she was restless and inattentive, and by and by leaving the artist talking to her young daughter she began going round by herself, moving constantly from picture to picture. Presently she made an exclamation, and turning they saw her standing before a picture, a portrait of a girl, staring fixedly at it. 'Oh,' she cried, and it was a cry of pain, 'was I once as beautiful as that?' and burst into tears. She had found the picture she had been looking for, which she had come to see; it had been there twenty to twenty-five years, and the story of it was as follows.

When she was a young girl her mother took her to the great artist to have her portrait painted, and when the work was at length fin-ished she and her mother went to see it. The artist put it before them and the mother looked at it, her face expressing displeasure, and said not one word. Nor did the artist open his lips. And at last the girl, to break the uncomfortable silence, said, 'Where shall we hang it, mother?' and the lady replied, 'Just where you like, my dear, so long as you hang it with the face to the wall.' It was an insolent, a cruel thing to say, but the artist did not answer her bitterly; he said gently that she need not take the portrait as it failed to please her, and that in any case he would decline to take the money she had agreed to pay him for the work. She thanked him coldly and went her way, and he never saw her again. And now Time, the humbler of proud beautiful women, had given him his revenge: the portrait, scorned and rejected when the colour and sparkle of life was in the face, had been looked on once more by its subject and had caused her to weep at the change in herself.

To return. One wishes in these moments of meeting, of surprise and sudden revealings, that it were permissible to speak from the heart, since then the very truth might have more balm than bitterness in it. 'Grieve not, dear friend of old days, that I have not escaped the illusion common to all – the idea that those we have not looked on this long time – full five years, let us say – have remained as they were while we ourselves have been moving onwards and downwards in that path in which our feet are set. No one, however hardened he may be, can escape a shock of surprise and pain; but now the illusion I cherished has gone – now I have seen with my physical eyes, and a new image, with Time's writing on it, has taken the place of the old and brighter one, I would not have it otherwise. No, not if I could would I call back the vanished lustre, since all these changes, above all that wistful look in the eyes, do but serve to make you dearer, my sister and friend and fellow-traveller in a land where we cannot find a permanent resting-place.'

Alas! it cannot be spoken, and we cannot comfort a sister if she cannot divine the thought; but to brood over these inevitable changes is as idle as it is to lament that we were born into this mutable world. After all, it is because of the losses, the sadnesses, that the world is so infinitely sweet to us. The thought is in Cory's *Mimnernus in Church*:

> All beauteous things for which we live
> By laws of time and space decay.
> But oh, the very reason why
> I clasp them is because they die.

From this sadness in Bath I went to a greater in Wells, where I had not been for ten years, and timing my visit so as to have a Sunday service at the cathedral of beautiful memories, I went on a Saturday to Shepton Mallet. A small, squalid town, a 'manufacturing town' the guide-books calls it. Well, yes; it manufactures Anglo-Bavarian beer in a gigantic brewery which looks bigger than all the other buildings together, the church and a dozen or twenty public-houses included. To get some food I went to the only eating-house in the place, and saw a pleasant-looking woman, plump and high-coloured, with black hair, with an expression of good humour and goodness of every description in her comely countenance. She promised to have a chop ready by the time I had finished looking at the church, and I said I would have it with a small Guinness.

She could not provide *that*, the house, she said, was *strictly* temperance. 'My doctor has ordered me to take it,' said I, 'and if you are religious, remember that St. Paul tells us to take a little stout when we find it beneficial.'

'Yes, I know that's what St. Paul says,' she returned, with a heightened colour and a vicious emphasis on the saint's name, 'but *we* go on a different principle.'

So I had to go for my lunch to one of the big public-houses, called hotels; but whether it called itself a cow, or horse, or stag, or angel, or a blue or green something, I cannot remember. They gave me what they called a beefsteak pie – a tough crust and under it some blackish cubes carved out of the muscle of an antediluvian ox-and for this delicious fare and a glass of stout I paid three shillings and odd pence.

As I came away Shepton Mallet was shaken to its foundations by a tremendous and most diabolical sound, a prolonged lupine yell or yowl, as if a stupendous wolf, as big, say, as the Anglo-Bavarian brewery, had howled his loudest and longest. This infernal row, which makes Shepton seem like a town or village gone raving mad, was merely to inform the men, and, incidentally, the universe, that it was time for them to knock off work.

Turning my back on the place, I said to myself, 'What a fool I am to be sure! Why could I not have been satisfied for once with a cup of coffee with my lunch? I should have saved a shilling, perhaps eighteen-pence, to rejoice the soul of some poor tramp; and, better still, I could have discussed some interesting questions with that charming rosy-faced woman. What, for instance, was the reason of her quarrel with the apostle; by the by, she never rebuked me for misquoting his words; and what is the moral effect (as seen through her clear brown eyes) of the Anglo-Bavarian brewery on the population of the small town and the neighbouring villages?'

The road I followed from Shepton to Wells winds by the water-side, a tributary of the Brue, in a narrow valley with hills on either side. It is a five-mile road through a beautiful country, where there is practically no cultivation, and the green hills, with brown woods in their hollows, and here and there huge masses of grey and reddish Bath stone cropping out on their sides, resembling gigantic castles and ramparts, long ruined and overgrown with ivy and bramble, produce the effect of a land dispeopled and gone back to a state of wildness.

A thaw had come that morning, ending the severest frost experienced this winter anywhere in England, and the valley was alive with birds, happy and tuneful at the end of January as in April. Looking down on the stream the sudden glory of a kingfisher passed before me; but the sooty-brown water-ouzel with his white bib, a haunter, too, of this water, I did not see. Within a mile or so of Wells I overtook a small boy who belonged there, and had been to Shepton like me, noticing the birds. 'I saw a kingfisher,' I said. 'So did I,' he returned quickly, with pride. He described it as a biggish bird with a long neck, but its colour was not blue – oh, no! I suggested that it was a heron, a long-necked creature under six feet high, of no particular colour. No, it was not a heron; and after taking thought, he said, 'I think it was a wild duck.'

Bestowing a penny to encourage him in his promising researches into the feathered world, I went on by a footpath over a hill, and as I mounted to the higher ground there before me rose the noble tower of St. Cuthbert's Church, and a little to the right of it, girt with high trees, the magnificent pile of the cathedral, with green hills and the pale sky beyond. O joy to look again on it, to add yet one more enduring image of it to the number I had long treasured! For the others were not exactly like this one; the building was not looked at from the same point of view at the same season and late hour, with the green hills lit by the departing sun and the clear pale winter sky beyond.

Coming in by the moated palace I stood once more on the Green before that west front, beautiful beyond all others, in spite of the strange defeatures Time has written on it. I watched the daws, numerous as ever, still at their old mad games, now springing into the air to scatter abroad with ringing cries, only to return the next minute and fling themselves back on their old perches on a hundred weather-stained broken statues in the niches. And while I stood watching them from the palace trees close by came the loud laugh of the green woodpecker. The same wild, beautiful sound, uttered perhaps by the same bird, which I had often heard at that spot ten years ago! 'You will not hear that woodland sound in any other city in the kingdom,' I wrote in a book of sketches entitled *Birds and Man*, published in 1901.

But of my soul's adventures in Wells on the two or three following days I will say very little. That laugh of the woodpecker was an assurance that Nature had suffered no change, and the town too, like the hills and rocks and running waters, seemed unchanged; but how different and how sad when I looked for those I once knew, whose hands I had hoped to grasp again! Yes, some were living still; and a dog too, one I used to take out for long walks and many a mad rabbit-hunt – a very handsome white-and-liver coloured spaniel. I found him lying on a sofa, and down he got and wagged his tail vigorously, pretending, with a pretty human hypocrisy in his gentle yellow eyes, that he knew me perfectly well, that I was not a bit changed, and that he was delighted to see me.

On my way back to Bath I had a day at Bristol. It was cattle-market day, and what with the bellowings, barkings, and shoutings, added to the buzz and clang of innumerable electric tramcars and the usual din of street traffic, one got the idea that the Bristolians had adopted a sort of Salvation Army theory, and were endeavouring to conquer earth (it is not heaven in this case) by making a tremendous noise. I amused myself strolling about and watching the people, and as train after train came in late in the day discharging loads of humanity, mostly young men and women from the surrounding country coming in for an evening's amusement, I noticed again the peculiarly Welsh character of the Somerset peasant – the shape of the face, the colour of the skin, and, above all, the expression.

Freeman, when here below, proclaimed it his mission to prove that 'Englishmen were Englishmen, and not somebody else.' It appeared to me that any person, unbiased by theories on such a subject, looking at that crowd, would have come to the conclusion, sadly or gladly, according to his nature, that we are, in fact, 'somebody else.'

CHAPTER FOURTEEN

The Return of the Native

That 'going back' about which I wrote in the second chapter to a place where an unexpected beauty or charm has revealed itself, and has made its image a lasting and prized possession of the mind, is not the same thing as the revisiting a famous town or city, rich in many beauties and old memories, such as Bath or Wells, for instance. Such centres have a permanent attraction, and one who is a rover in the land must return to them again and again, nor does he fail on each successive visit to find some fresh charm or interest. The sadness of such returns, after a long interval, is only, as I have said, when we start 'looking up' those with whom we had formed pleasant friendly relations. And all because of the illusion that we shall see them as they were – that Time has stood still waiting for our return, and by and by, to our surprise and grief, we discover that it is not so; that the dear friends of other days, long unvisited but unforgotten, have become strangers. This human loss is felt even more in the case of a return to some small centre, a village or hamlet where we knew everyone, and our intimacy with the people has produced the sense of being one in blood with them. It is greatest of all when we return to a childhood's or boyhood's home. Many writers have occupied themselves with this mournful theme, and I imagine that a person of the proper Amiel-like tender and melancholy moralizing type of mind, by using his own and his friends' experiences, could write a charmingly sad and pretty book on the subject.

The really happy returns of this kind must be exceedingly rare. I am almost surprised to think that I am able to recall as many as two, but they hardly count, as in both instances the departure or exile from home happens at so early a time of life that no recollections of the people survived – nothing, in fact, but a vague mental picture of the place. One was of a business man I knew in London, who lost his early home in a village in the Midlands, as a boy of eight or nine years of age, through the sale of the place by his father, who had become impoverished. The boy was trained to business in London, and when a middle-aged man, wishing to retire and spend the rest of his life in the country, he revisited his native village for the first time, and discovered to his joy that he could buy back the old home. He was, when I last saw him, very happy in its possession.

The other case I will relate more fully, as it is a very curious one, and came to my knowledge in a singular way.

At a small station near Eastleigh a man wearing a highly pleased expression on his face entered the smoking-carriage in which I was travelling to London. Putting his bag on the rack, he pulled out his pipe and threw himself back in his seat with a satisfied air; then, looking at me and catching my eye, he at once started talking. I had my newspaper, but seeing him in that overflowing mood I responded readily enough, for I was curious to know why he appeared so happy and who and what he was. Not a tradesman nor a bagman, and not a farmer, though he looked like an open-air man; nor could I form a guess from his speech and manner as to his native place. A robust man of thirty-eight or forty, with blue eyes and a Saxon face, he looked a thorough Englishman, and yet he struck me as most un-English in his lively, almost eager manner, his freedom with a stranger, and something, too, in his speech. From time to time his face lighted up, when, looking to the window, his eyes rested on some pretty scene – a glimpse of stately old elm trees in a field where cattle were grazing, of the vivid green valley of a chalk stream, the paler hills beyond, the grey church tower or spire of some tree-hidden village. When he discovered that these hills and streams and rustic villages had as great a charm for me as for himself, that I knew and loved the two or three places he named in a questioning way, he opened his heart and the secret of his present happiness.

He was a native of the district, born at a farmhouse of which his father in succession to his grandfather had been the tenant. It was a small farm of only eighty-five acres, and as his father could make no more than a bare livelihood out of it, he eventually gave it up when my informant was but three years old, and selling all he had, emigrated to Australia. Nine years later he died, leaving a numerous family poorly provided for; the home was broken up and boys and girls had to go out and face the world. They had somehow all got on very well, and his brothers and sisters were happy enough out there, Australians in mind, thoroughly persuaded that theirs was the better land, the best country in the world, and with no desire to visit England. He had never felt like that; somehow his father's feeling about the old country had taken such a hold of him that he never outlived it – never felt at home in Australia, however successful he was in his affairs. The home feeling had been very strong in his father; his greatest delight was to sit of an evening with his children round him and tell them of the farm and the old farm-house where he was born and had lived so many years, and where some of them too had been born. He was never tired of talking of it, of taking them by the hand, as it were, and leading them from place to place, to the stream, the village, the old stone church, the meadows and fields and hedges, the deep shady lanes, and, above all, to the dear old ivied house with its gables and tall chimneys. So many times had his father described it that the old place was printed like a map on his mind, and was like a picture which kept its brightness even after the image of his boyhood's home in Australia had become faded and pale. With that mental picture to guide him he believed that he could go to that angle by the porch where the flycatchers bred every year and find their nest; where in the hedge the blackberries were most abundant; where the elders grew by the stream from which he could watch the moorhens and watervoles; that he knew every fence, gate, and outhouse, every room and passage in the old house. Through all his busy years that picture never grew less beautiful, never ceased its call, and at last, possessed of sufficient capital to yield him a modest income for the rest of his life, he came home. What he was going to do in England he did not consider. He only knew that until he had satisfied the chief desire of his heart and had looked upon the original of the picture he had borne so long in his mind he could not rest nor make any plans for the future.

He came first to London and found, on examining the map of Hampshire, that the village of Thorpe (I will call it), where he was born, is three miles from the nearest station, in the southern part of the county. Undoubtedly it was Thorpe; that was one of the few names of places his father had mentioned which remained in his memory always associated with that vivid image of the farm in his mind. To Thorpe he accordingly went – as pretty a rustic village as he had hoped to find it. He took a room at the inn and went out for a long walk – 'just to see the place,' he said to the landlord. He would make no inquiries; he would find his home for himself; how could he fail to recognize it? But he walked for hours in a widening circle and saw no farm or other house, and no ground that corresponded to the picture in his brain.

Troubled at his failure, he went back and questioned his landlord, and, naturally, was asked for the name of the farm he was seeking. He had forgotten the name – he even doubted that he had ever heard it. But there was his family name to go by – Dyson; did any one remember a farmer Dyson in the village? He was told that it was not an uncommon name in that part of the country. There were no Dysons now in Thorpe, but some fifteen or twenty years ago one of that name had been the tenant of Long Meadow Farm in the parish. The name of the farm was unfamiliar, and when he visited the place he found it was not the one he sought.

It was a grievous disappointment. A new sense of loneliness oppressed him; for that bright image in his mind, with the feeling about his home, had been a secret source of comfort and happiness, and was like a companion, a dear human friend, and now he appeared to be on the point of losing it. Could it be that all that mental picture, with the details that seemed so true to life, was purely imaginary? He could not believe it; the old house had probably been pulled down, the big trees felled, orchard and hedges grabbed up – all the old features obliterated – and the land thrown into some larger neighbouring farm. It was dreadful to think that such devastating changes had been made, but it had certainly existed as he saw it in his mind, and he would inquire of some of the old men in the place, who would perhaps be able to tell him where his home had stood thirty years ago.

At once he set about interviewing all the old men he came upon in his rounds, describing to them the farm tenanted by a man named Dyson about forty years ago, and by and by he got hold of one who knew. He listened for a few minutes to the oft-repeated story, then exclaimed, 'Why, sir, 'tis surely Woodyates you be talking about!'

'That's the name! That's the name,' he cried. 'Woodyates-how did I ever forget it! You knew it then – where was it?'

'I'll just show you,' said the old man, proud at having guessed rightly, and turning started slowly hobbling along till he got to the end of the lane.

There was an opening there and a view of the valley with trees, blue in the distance, at the furthest visible point. 'Do you see them trees?' he said. 'That's where Harping is; 'tis two miles or, perhaps, a little more from Thorpe. There's a church tower among them trees, but you can't see it because 'tis hid. You go by the road till you comes to the church, then you go on by the water, maybe a quarter of a mile, and you comes to Woodyates. You won't see no difference in it; I've knowed it since I were a boy, but 'tis in Harping parish, not in Thorpe.'

Now he remembered the name – Harping, near Thorpe – only Thorpe was the more important village where the inn was and the shops.

In less than an hour after leaving his informant he was at Woodyates, feasting his eyes on the old house of his dreams and of his exiled father's before him, inexpressibly glad to recognize it as the very house he had loved so long – that he had been deceived by no false image.

For some days he haunted the spot, then became a lodger at the farm-house, and now after making some inquiries he had found that the owner was willing to sell the place for something more than its market value, and he was going up to London about it.

At Waterloo I wished him happiness in his old home found again after so many years, then watched him as he walked briskly away – as commonplace-looking a man as could be seen on that busy crowded platform, in his suit of rough grey tweeds, thick boots, and bowler hat. Yet one whose fortune might be envied by many even among the successful – one who had cherished a secret thought and feeling, which had been to him like the shadow of a rock and like a cool spring in a dry and thirsty land.

And in that host of undistinguished Colonials and others of British race from all regions of the earth, who annually visit these shores on business or for pleasure or some other object, how many there must be who come with some such memory or dream or aspiration in their hearts! A greater number probably than we imagine. For most of them there is doubtless disappointment and disillusion: it is a matter of the heart, a sentiment about which some are not given to speak. He too, my fellow-passenger, would no doubt have held his peace had his dream not met with so perfect a fulfilment. As it was he had to tell his joy to someone, though it were to a stranger.

CHAPTER FIFTEEN

Summer Days on the Otter

The most characteristic district of South Devon, the greenest, most luxuriant in its vegetation, and perhaps the hottest in England, is that bit
of country between the Exe and the Axe which is watered by the Clyst,
the Otter, and the Sid. In any one of a dozen villages found beside these
pretty little rivers a man might spend a month, a year, a lifetime, very
agreeably, ceasing not to congratulate himself on the good fortune which
first led him into such a garden. Yet after a week or two in this luxurious
land I began to be dissatisfied with my surroundings. It was June; the
weather was exceptionally dry and sultry. Vague thoughts, or 'visitings'
of mountains and moors and coasts would intrude to make the confinement of deep lanes seem increasingly irksome. Each day I wandered
miles in some new direction, never knowing whither the devious path
would lead me, never inquiring of any person, nor consulting map or
guide, since to do that is to deprive oneself of the pleasure of discovery;
always with a secret wish to find some exit as it were – some place
beyond the everlasting wall of high hedges and green trees, where there
would be a wide horizon and wind blowing unobstructed over leagues
of open country to bring me back the sense of lost liberty. I found only
fresh woods and pastures new that were like the old; other lanes leading
to other farm-houses, each in its familiar pretty setting of orchard and
garden; and, finally, other ancient villages, each with its ivy-grown grey
church tower looking down on a green graveyard and scattered cottages, mostly mud-built and thatched with straw. Finding no outlook on
any side I went back to the streams, oftenest to the Otter, where, lying
by the hour on the bank, I watched the speckled trout below me and the
dark-plumaged dipper with shining white breast standing solitary and
curtseying on a stone in the middle of the current. Sometimes a kingfisher would flash by, and occasionally I came upon a lonely grey heron;
but no mammal bigger than a watervole appeared, although I waited
and watched for the much bigger beast that gives the river its name. Still
it was good to know that he was there, and had his den somewhere in
the steep rocky bank under the rough tangle of ivy and bramble and
roots of overhanging trees. One was shot by a farmer during my stay,
but my desire was for the living, not a dead otter. Consequently, when

the otter-hunt came with blaze of scarlet coats and blowing of brass horns and noise of barking hounds and shouts of excited people, it had no sooner got half a mile above Ottery St. Mary, where I had joined the straggling procession, than, falling behind, the hunting fury died out of me and I was relieved to hear that no quarry had been found. The frightened moorhen stole back to her spotty eggs, the dipper returned to his dipping and curtseying to his own image in the stream, and I to my idle dreaming and watching.

The watching was not wholly in vain, since there were here revealed to me things, or aspects of things, that were new. A great deal depends on atmosphere and the angle of vision. For instance, I have often looked at swans at the hour of sunset, on the water and off it, or flying, and have frequently had them between me and the level sun, yet never have I been favoured with the sight of the rose-coloured, the red, and the golden-yellow varieties of that majestic waterfowl, whose natural colour is white. On the other hand, who ever saw a carrion-crow with crimson eyes? Yet that was one of the strange things I witnessed on the Otter.

Game is not everywhere strictly preserved in that part of Devon, and the result is that the crow is not so abhorred and persecuted a fowl as in many places, especially in the home counties, where the cult of the sacred bird is almost universal. At one spot on the stream where my rambles took me on most days a pair of crows invariably greeted my approach with a loud harsh remonstrance, and would keep near me, flying from tree to tree repeating their angry girdings until I left the place. Their nest was in a large elm, and after some days I was pleased to see that the young had been safely brought off. The old birds screamed at me no more; then I came on one of their young in the meadow near the river. His curious behaviour interested me so much that I stood and watched him for half an hour or longer. It was a hot, windless day, and the bird was by himself among the tall flowering grasses and buttercups of the meadow – a queer gaunt unfinished hobbledehoy-looking fowl with a head much too big for his body, a beak that resembled a huge nose, and a very monstrous mouth. When I first noticed him he was amusing himself by picking off the small insects from the flowers with his big beak, a most unsuitable instrument, one would imagine, for so delicate a task. At the same time he was hungering for more substantial fare, and every time a rook flew by over him on its way to or from a neighbouring too populous rookery, the young crow would open wide his immense red mouth and emit his harsh, throaty hunger-call. The rook gone, he would drop once more into his study of the buttercups, to pick from them whatever unconsidered trifle in the way of provender he could find. Once a small bird, a pied wagtail, flew near him, and he begged from it just as he had done from the rooks: the little creature would have run the risk of being itself swallowed had it attempted to deliver a packet of flies into that cavernous mouth. I went nearer, moving cautiously, until I was within about four yards of him, when, half turning, he opened his mouth and squawked, actually asking *me* to feed him; then, growing suspicious, he hopped awkwardly away in the grass. Eventually he permitted a nearer approach, and slowly stooping I was just on the point of stroking his back when, suddenly becoming alarmed, he swung himself into the air and flapped laboriously off to a low hawthorn, twenty or thirty yards away, into which he tumbled pell-mell like a bundle of old black rags.

Then I left him and thought no more about the crows except that their young have a good deal to learn upon first coming forth into an unfriendly world. But there was a second nest and family close by all the time. A day or two later I discovered it accidentally in a very curious way.

There was one spot where I was accustomed to linger for a few minutes, sometimes for half an hour or so, during my daily walks. Here at the foot of the low bank on the treeless side of the stream there was a scanty patch of sedges, a most exposed and unsuitable place for any bird to breed in, yet a venturesome moorhen had her nest there and was now sitting on seven eggs. First I would take a peep at the eggs, for the bird always quitted the nest on my approach; then I would gaze into the dense tangle of tree, bramble, and ivy springing out of the mass of black rock and red clay of the opposite bank. In the centre of this rough tangle which overhung the stream there grew an old stunted and crooked fir tree with its tufted top so shut out from the light by the branches and foliage round it that it looked almost black. One evening I sat down on the green bank opposite this tangle when the low sun behind me shone level into the mass of rock and rough boles and branches, and fixing my eyes on the black centre of the mass I encountered a pair of crimson eyes staring back into mine. A level ray of light had lit up that spot which I had always seen in deep shadow, revealing its secret. After gazing steadily for some time I made out a crow's nest in the dwarf pine top and the vague black forms of three young fully fledged crows sitting or standing in it. The middle bird had the shining crimson eyes; but in a few moments the illusory colour was gone and the eyes were black.

It was certainly an extraordinary thing: the ragged-looking black-plumaged bird on its ragged nest of sticks in the deep shade, with one ray of intense sunlight on its huge nose-like beak and blood-red eyes, a sight to be remembered for a lifetime! It recalled Zurbaran's picture of the 'Kneeling Monk,' in which the man with everything about him is steeped in the deepest gloom except his nose, on which one ray of strong light has fallen. The picture of the monk is gloomy and austere in a wonderful degree: the crow in his interior with sunlit big beak and crimson eyes looked nothing less than diabolical.

I paid other visits to the spot at the same hour, and sat long and watched the crows while they watched me, occasionally tossing pebbles on to them to make them shift their positions, but the magical effect was not produced again.

As to the cause of that extraordinary colour in the crow's eyes, one might say that it was merely the reflected red light of the level sun. We are familiar with the effect when polished and wet surfaces, such as glass, stone, and water, shine crimson in the light of a setting sun; but there is also the fact, which is not well known, that the eye may show its own hidden red – the crimson colour which is at the back of the retina and which is commonly supposed to be seen only with the ophthalmoscope. Nevertheless I find on inquiry among friends and acquaintances that there are instances of persons in which the iris when directly in front of the observer with the light behind him, always looks crimson, and in several of these cases the persons exhibiting this colour, or danger signal, as it may be called, were subject to brain trouble. It is curious to find that the crimson colour or light has also been observed in dogs: one friend has told me of a pet King Charles, a lively good-tempered little dog with brown eyes like any other dog, which yet when they looked up into yours in a room always shone ruby-red instead of hyaline blue, or green, as is usually the case. From other friends I heard of many other cases: one was of a child, an infant in arms, whose eyes sometimes appeared crimson, another of a cat with yellow eyes which shone crimson-red in certain lights. Of human adults, I heard of two men great in the world of science, both dead now, in whose eyes the red light had been seen just before and during attacks of nervous breakdown. I heard also of four other persons, not distinguished in any way, two of them sisters, who showed the red light in the eyes: all of them suffered from brain trouble and two of them ended their lives in asylums for the insane.

Discussing these cases with my informants, we came to the conclusion that the red light in the human eye is probably always a pathological condition, a danger signal; but it is not perhaps safe to generalize on these few instances, and I must add that all the medical men I have spoken to on the subject shake their heads. One great man, an eye specialist, went so far as to say that it is impossible, that the red light in the eye was not seen by my informants but only imagined. The ophthalmoscope, he said, will show you the crimson at the back of the eye, but the colour is not and cannot be reflected on the surface of the iris.

CHAPTER SIXTEEN

In Praise of the Cow

In spite of discontents I might have remained to this day by the Otter, in the daily and hourly expectation of seeing some new and wonderful thing in Nature in that place where a crimson-eyed carrion-crow had been revealed to me, had not a storm of thunder and rain broken over the country to shake me out of a growing disinclination to move. We are, body and mind, very responsive to atmospheric changes; for every storm in Nature there is a storm in us – a change physical and mental. We make our own conditions, it is true, and these react and have a deadening effect on us in the long run, but we are never wholly deadened by them – if we be not indeed dead, if the life we live can be called life. We are told that there are rainless zones on the earth and regions of everlasting summer: it is hard to believe that the dwellers in such places can ever think a new thought or do a new thing.

The morning rain did not last very long, and before it had quite ceased I took up my knapsack and set off towards the sea, determined on this occasion to make my escape.

Three or four miles from Ottery St. Mary I overtook a cowman driving nine milch cows along a deep lane and inquired my way of him. He gave me many and minute directions, after which we got into conversation, and I walked some distance with him.

The cows he was driving were all pure Devons, perfect beauties in their bright red coats in that greenest place where every rain-wet leaf sparkled in the new sunlight. Naturally we talked about the cows, and I soon found that they were his own and the pride and joy of his life. We walked leisurely, and as the animals went on, first one, then another would stay for a mouthful of grass, or to pull down half a yard of green drapery from the hedge. It was so lavishly decorated that the damage they did to it was not noticeable. By and by we went on ahead of the cows, then, if one stayed too long or strayed into some inviting side-lane, he would turn and utter a long, soft call, whereupon the straggler would leave her browsing and hasten after the others.

He was a big, strongly built man, a little past middle life and grey-haired, with rough-hewn face – unprepossessing one would have pronounced him until the intelligent, kindly expression of the eyes was seen and the agreeable voice was heard. As our talk progressed and we found how much in sympathy we were on the subject, I was reminded of that Biblical expression about the shining of a man's face: 'Wine that maketh glad the heart of man' – I hope the total abstainers will pardon me – 'and oil that maketh his face to shine,' we have in one passage. This rather goes against our British ideas, since we rub no oil or unguents on our skin, but only soap which deprives it of its natural oil and too often imparts a dry and hard texture. Yet in that, to us, disagreeable aspect of the skin caused by foreign fats, there is a resemblance to the sudden brightening and glory of the countenance in moments of blissful emotion or exaltation. No doubt the effect is produced by the eyes, which are the mirrors of the mind, and as they are turned full upon us they produce an illusion, seeming to make the whole face shine.

In our talk I told him of long rambles on the Mendips, along the valley of the Somerset Axe, where I had lately been, and where of all places in this island, the cow should be most esteemed and loved by man. Yet even there, where, standing on some elevation, cows beyond one's power to number could be seen scattered far and wide in the green vales beneath, it had saddened me to find them so silent. It is not natural for them to be dumb; they have great emotions and mighty voices – the cattle on a thousand hills. Their morning and evening lowing is more to me than any other natural sound – the melody of birds, the springs and dying gales of the pines, the wash of waves on the long shingled beach. The hills and valleys of that pastoral country flowing with milk and honey should be vocal with it, echoing and re-echoing the long call made musical by distance. The cattle are comparatively silent in that beautiful district, and indeed everywhere in England, because men have made them so. They have, when deprived of their calves, no motive for the exercise of their voices. For two or three days after their new-born calves have been taken from them they call loudly and incessantly, day and night, like Rachel weeping for her children and refusing to be comforted; grief and anxiety inspires that cry – they grow hoarse with crying; it is a powerful, harsh, discordant sound, unlike the long musical call of the cow that has a calf, and remembering it, and leaving the pasture, goes lowing to give it suck.

I also told him of the cows of a distant country where I had lived, that had the maternal instinct so strong that they refused to yield their milk when deprived of their young. They 'held it back,' as the saying is, and were in a sullen rage, and in a few days their fountains dried up, and there was no more milk until calving-time came round once more.

He replied that cows of that temper were not unknown in South Devon. Very proudly he pointed to one of the small herd that followed us as an example. In most cases, he said, the calf was left from two or three days to a week, or longer, with the mother to get strong, and then taken away. This plan could not be always followed; some cows were so greatly distressed at losing the young they had once suckled that precautions had to be taken and the calf smuggled away as quietly as possible when dropped – if possible before the mother had seen it. Then there were the extreme cases in which the cow refused to be cheated. She knew that a calf had been born; she had felt it within her, and had suffered pangs in bringing it forth; if it appeared not on the grass or straw at her side then it must have been snatched away by the human creatures that hovered about her, like crows and ravens round a ewe in travail on some lonely mountain side. That was the character of the cow he had pointed out; even when she had not seen the calf of which she had been deprived she made so great an outcry and was thrown into such a rage and fever, refusing to be milked, that, finally, to save her, it was thought necessary to give her back the calf. Now, he concluded, it was not attempted to take it away: twice a day she was allowed to have it with her and suckle it, and she was a very happy animal.

I was glad to think that there was at least one completely happy cow in Devonshire.

After leaving the cowkeeper I had that feeling of revulsion very strongly which all who know and love cows occasionally experience at the very thought of beef. I was for the moment more than tolerant of vegetarianism, and devoutly hoped that for many days to come I should not be sickened with the sight of a sirloin on some hateful board, cold, or smoking hot, bleeding its red juices into the dish when gashed with a knife, as if undergoing a second death. We do not eat negroes, although their pigmented skins, flat feet, and woolly heads proclaim them a different species; even monkey's flesh is abhorrent to us, merely because we fancy that that creature in its ugliness resembles some old men and some women and children that we know. But the gentle large-brained social cow that caresses our hands and faces with her rough blue tongue, and is more like man's sister than any other non-human being – the majestic, beautiful creature with the Juno eyes, sweeter of breath than the rosiest virgin – we slaughter and feed on her flesh – monsters and cannibals that we are!

But though cannibals, it is very pleasant to find that many cowmen love their cows. Walking one afternoon by a high unkept hedge near Southampton Water, I heard loud shouts at intervals issuing from a point some distance ahead, and on arriving at the spot found an old man leaning idly over a gate, apparently concerned about nothing. 'What are you shouting about?' I demanded. 'Cows,' he answered, with a glance across the wide green field dotted with a few big furze and bramble bushes. On its far side half a dozen cows were quietly grazing. 'They came fast enough when I was a-feeding of 'em,' he presently added; 'but now they has to fend for theirselves they don't care how long they keeps me.' I was going to suggest that it would be a considerable saving of time if he went for them, but his air of lazy contentment as he leant on the gate showed that time was of no importance to him. He was a curious-looking old man, in old frayed clothes, broken boots, and a cap too small for him. He had short legs, broad chest, and long arms, and a very big head, long and horselike, with a large shapeless nose and grizzled beard and moustache. His ears, too, were enormous, and stood out from the head like the handles of a rudely shaped terracotta vase or jar. The colour of his face, the ears included, suggested burnt clay. But though Nature had made him ugly, he had an agreeable expression, a sweet benign look in his large dark eyes, which attracted me, and I stayed to talk with him.

It has frequently been said that those who are much with cows, and have an affection for them, appear to catch something of their expression – to look like cows; just as persons of sympathetic or responsive nature, and great mobility of face, grow to be like those they live and are in sympathy with. The cowman who looks like a cow may be more bovine than his fellows in his heavier motions and slower apprehensions, but he also exhibits some of the better qualities – the repose and placidity of the animal.

He said that he was over seventy, and had spent the whole of his life in the neighbourhood, mostly with cows, and had never been more than a dozen miles from the spot where we were standing. At intervals while we talked he paused to utter one of his long shouts, to which the cows paid no attention. At length one of the beasts raised her head and had a long look, then slowly crossed the field to us, the others following at some distance. They were shorthorns, all but the leader, a beautiful young Devon, of a uniform rich glossy red; but the silky hair on the distended udder was of an intense chestnut, and all the parts that were not clothed were red too – the teats, the skin round the eyes, the moist embossed nose; while the hoofs were like polished red pebbles, and even the shapely horns were tinged with that colour. Walking straight up to the old man, she began deliberately licking one of his ears with her big rough tongue, and in doing so knocked off his old rakish cap. Picking it up he laughed like a child, and remarked, 'She knows me, this one does – and she loikes me.'

CHAPTER SEVENTEEN

An Old Road Leading Nowhere

So many and minute were the directions I received about the way from the blessed cowkeeper, and so little attention did I give them, my mind being occupied with other things, that they were quickly forgotten. Of half a hundred things I remembered only that I had to 'bear to the left.' This I did, although it seemed useless, seeing that my way was by lanes, across fields, and through plantations. At length I came to a road, and as it happened to be on my left hand I followed it. It was narrow, worn deep by traffic and rains; and grew deeper, rougher, and more untrodden as I progressed, until it was like the dry bed of a mountain torrent, and I walked on boulder-stones between steep banks about fourteen feet high. Their sides were clothed with ferns, grass and rank moss; their summits were thickly wooded, and the interlacing branches of the trees above, mingled with long rope-like shoots of bramble and briar, formed so close a roof that I seemed to be walking in a dimly lighted tunnel. At length, thinking that I had kept long enough to a road which had perhaps not been used for a century, also tired of the monotony of always bearing to the left, I scrambled out on the right-hand side. For some time past I had been ascending a low, broad, flat-topped hill, and on forcing my way through the undergrowth into the open I found myself on the level plateau, an unenclosed spot overgrown with heather and scattered furze bushes, with clumps of fir and birch trees. Before me and on either hand at this elevation a vast extent of country was disclosed. The surface was everywhere broken, but there was no break in the wonderful greenness, which the recent rain had intensified. There is too much green, to my thinking, with too much uniformity in its soft, bright tone, in South Devon. After gazing on such a landscape the brown, harsh, scanty vegetation of the hilltop seemed all the more grateful. The heath was an oasis and a refuge; I rambled about in it until my feet and legs were wet; then I sat down to let them dry and altogether spent several agreeable hours at that spot, pleased at the thought that no human fellow-creature would intrude upon me. Feathered companions were, however, not wanting. The crowing of cock pheasants from the thicket beside the old road warned me that

I was on preserved grounds. Not too strictly preserved, however, for there was my old friend the carrion-crow out foraging for his young. He dropped down over the trees, swept past me, and was gone. At this season, in the early summer, he may be easily distinguished, when flying, from his relation the rook. When on the prowl the crow glides smoothly and rapidly through the air, often changing his direction, now flying close to the surface, anon mounting high, but oftenest keeping nearly on a level with the tree tops. His gliding and curving motions are somewhat like those of the herring-gull, but the wings in gliding are carried stiff and straight, the tips of the long flight-feathers showing a slight upward curve. But the greatest difference is in the way the head is carried. The rook, like the heron and stork, carries his beak pointing lance-like straight before him. He knows his destination, and makes for it; he follows his nose, so to speak, turning neither to the right nor the left. The foraging crow continually turns his head, gull-like and harrier-like, from side to side, as if to search the ground thoroughly or to concentrate his vision on some vaguely seen object.

Not only the crow was there: a magpie chattered as I came from the brake, but refused to show himself; and a little later a jay screamed at me, as only a jay can. There are times when I am intensely in sympathy with the feeling expressed in this ear-splitting sound, inarticulate but human. It is at the same time warning and execration, the startled solitary's outburst of uncontrolled rage at the abhorred sight of a fellow-being in his woodland haunt.

Small birds were numerous at that spot, as if for them also its wildness and infertility had an attraction. Tits, warblers, pipits, finches, all were busy ranging from place to place, emitting their various notes now from the tree-tops, then from near the ground; now close at hand, then far off; each change in the height, distance, and position of the singer giving the sound a different character, so that the effect produced was one of infinite variety. Only the yellow-hammer remained constant in one spot, in one position, and the song at each repetition was the same. Nevertheless this bird is not so monotonous a singer as he is reputed. A lover of open places, of commons and waste lands, with a bush or dwarf tree for tower to sit upon, he is yet one of the most common species in the thickly timbered country of the Otter, Clyst, and Sid, in which I had been rambling, hearing him every day and all day long. Throughout that district, where the fields are small, and the trees big and near together, he has the cirl-bunting's habit of perching to sing on the tops of high hedgerow elms and oaks.

By and by I had a better bird to listen to – a redstart. A female flew down within fifteen yards of me; her mate followed and perched on a dry twig, where he remained a long time for so shy and restless a creature. He was in perfect plumage, and sitting there, motionless in the strong sunlight, was wonderfully conspicuous, the gayest, most exotic-looking bird of his family in England. Quitting his perch, he flew up into a tree close by and began singing; and for half an hour thereafter I continued intently listening to his brief strain, repeated at short intervals – a song which I think has never been perfectly described. 'Practice makes perfect' is an axiom that does not apply to the art of song in the bird world; since the redstart, a member of a highly melodious family, with a good voice to start with, has never attained to excellence in spite of much practising. The song is interesting both on account of its exceptional inferiority and of its character. A distinguished ornithologist has said that little birds have two ways of making themselves attractive – by melody and by bright plumage; and that most species excel in one or the other way; and that the acquisition of gay colours by a species of a sober-coloured melodious family will cause it to degenerate as a songster. He is speaking of the redstart. Unfortunately for the rule there are too many exceptions. Thus confining ourselves to a single family – that of the finches – in our own islands, the most modest coloured have the least melody, while those that have the gayest plumage are the best singers – the goldfinch, chaffinch, siskin, and linnet. Nevertheless it is impossible to listen for any length of time to the redstart, and to many redstarts, without feeling, almost with irritation, that its strain is only the prelude of a song – a promise never performed; that once upon a time in the remote past it was a sweet, copious, and varied singer, and that only a fragment of its melody now remains. The opening rapidly warbled notes are so charming that the attention is instantly attracted by them. They are composed of two sounds, both beautiful – the bright pure gushing robin-like note, and the more tender expressive swallow-like note. And that is all; the song scarcely begins before it ends, or collapses; for in most cases the pure sweet opening strain is followed by a curious little farrago of gurgling and squeaking sounds, and little fragments of varied notes, often so low as to be audible only at a few yards' distance. It is curious that these slight fragments of notes at the end vary in different individuals, in strength and character and in number, from a single faintest squeal to half a dozen or a dozen distinct sounds. In all cases they are emitted with apparent effort, as if the bird strained its pipe in the vain attempt to continue the song.

The statement that the redstart is a mimic is to be met with in many books about birds. I rather think that in jerking out these various little broken notes which end its strain, whether he only squeaks or succeeds in producing a pure sound, he is striving to recover his own lost song rather than to imitate the songs of other birds.

So much entertainment did I find at that spot, so grateful did it seem in its openness after long confinement in the lower thickly wooded country, that I practically spent the day there. At all events the best time for walking was gone when I quitted it, and then I could think of no better plan than to climb down into the old long untrodden road, or channel, again just to see where it would lead me. After all, I said, my time is my own, and to abandon the old way I have walked in so long without discovering the end would be a mistake. So I went on in it once more, and in about twenty minutes it came to an end before a group of old farm buildings in a hollow in the woods. The space occupied by the buildings was quite walled round and shut in by a dense growth of trees and bushes; and there was no soul there and no domestic animal. The place had apparently been vacant many years, and the buildings were in a ruinous condition, with the roofs falling in.

Now when I look back on that walk I blame myself for having gone on my way without trying to find out something of the history of that forsaken home to which the lonely old road had led me. Those ruinous buildings once inhabited, so wrapped round and hidden away by trees, have now a strange look in memory as if they had a story to tell, as if something intelligent had looked from the vacant windows as I stood staring at them and had said, We have waited these many years for you to come and listen to our story and you are come at last.

Something perhaps stirred in me in response to that greeting and message, but I failed to understand it, and after standing there awhile, oppressed by a sense of loneliness, I turned aside, and creeping and pushing through a mass and tangle of vegetation went on my way towards the coast.

Possibly that idea or fancy of a story to tell, a human tragedy, came to me only because of another singular experience I had that day when the afternoon sun had grown oppressively hot – another mystery of a desolate but not in this case uninhabited house. The two places somehow became associated together in my mind.

The place was a little farm-house standing some distance from the road, in a lonely spot out of sight of any other habitation, and I thought I would call and ask for a glass of milk, thinking that if things had a promising look on my arrival my modest glass of milk would perhaps expand to a sumptuous five-o'clock tea and my short rest to a long and pleasant one.

The house I found on coming nearer was small and mean-looking and very old; the farm buildings in a dilapidated condition, the thatch rotten and riddled with holes in which many starlings and sparrows had their nests. Gates and fences were broken down, and the ground was everywhere overgrown with weeds and encumbered with old broken and rusty implements, and littered with rubbish. No person could I see about the place, but knew it was inhabited as there were some fowls walking about, and some calves shut in a pen in one of the numerous buildings were dolefully calling – calling to be fed. Seeing a door half open at one end of the house I went to it and rapped on the warped paintless wood with my stick, and after about a minute a young woman came from an inner room and asked me what I wanted. She was not disturbed or surprised at my sudden appearance there: her face was impassive, and her eyes when they met mine appeared to look not at me but at something distant, and her words were spoken mechanically.

I said that I was hot and thirsty and tired and would be glad of a glass of milk.

Without a word she turned and left me standing there, and presently returned with a tumbler of milk which she placed on a deal table standing near me. To my remarks she replied in monosyllables, and stood impassively, her hands at her side, her eyes cast down, waiting for me to drink the milk and go. And when I had finished it and set the glass down and thanked her, she turned in silence and went back to that inner room from which she first came. And hot and tired as I had felt a few moments before, and desirous of an interval of rest in the cool shade, I was glad to be out in the burning sun once more, for the sight of that young woman had chilled my blood and made the heat out-of-doors seem grateful to me.

The sight of such a face in the midst of such surroundings had produced a shock of surprise, for it was noble in shape, the features all fine and the mouth most delicately chiselled, the eyes dark and beautiful, and the hair of a raven blackness. But it was a colourless face, and even the lips were pale. Strongest of all was the expression, which had frozen there, and was like the look of one on whom some unimaginable disaster or some hateful disillusionment had come, not to subdue nor soften, but to change all its sweet to sour, and its natural warmth to icy cold.

CHAPTER EIGHTEEN

Branscombe

Health and pleasure resorts and all parasitic towns in fact, inland or on the sea, have no attractions for me and I was more than satisfied with a day or two of Sidmouth. Then one evening I heard for the first time of a place called Branscombe – a village near the sea, over by Beer and Seaton, near the mouth of the Axe, and the account my old host gave me seemed so attractive that on the following day I set out to find it. Further information about the unknown village came to me in a very agreeable way in the course of my tramp. A hotter walk I never walked – no, not even when travelling across a flat sunburnt treeless plain, nearer than Devon by many degrees to the equator. One wonders why that part of Devon which lies between the Exe and the Axe seems actually hotter than other regions which undoubtedly have a higher temperature. After some hours of walking with not a little of uphill and downhill, I began to find the heat well-nigh intolerable. I was on a hard dusty glaring road, shut in by dusty hedges on either side. Not a breath of air was stirring; not a bird sang; on the vast sky not a cloud appeared. If the vertical sun had poured down water instead of light and heat on me my clothing could not have clung to me more uncomfortably. Coming at length to a group of two or three small cottages at the roadside, I went into one and asked for something to quench my thirst – cider or milk. There was only water to be had, but it was good to drink, and the woman of the cottage was so pretty and pleasant that I was glad to rest an hour and talk with her in her cool kitchen. There are English counties where it would perhaps be said of such a woman that she was one in a thousand; but the Devonians are a comely race. In that blessed county the prettiest peasants are not all diligently gathered with the dew on them and sent away to supply the London flower-market. Among the best-looking women of the peasant class there are two distinct types – the rich in colour and the colourless. A majority are perhaps intermediate, but the two extreme types may be found in any village or hamlet; and when seen side by side – the lily and the rose, not to say the peony – they offer a strange and beautiful contrast.

This woman, in spite of the burning climate, was white as any pale town lady; and although she was the mother of several children, the face was extremely youthful in appearance; it seemed indeed almost girlish in its delicacy and innocent expression when she looked up at me with her blue eyes shaded by her white sun-bonnet. The children were five or six in number, ranging from a boy of ten to a baby in her arms – all clean and healthy looking, with bright, fun-loving faces.

I mentioned that I was on my way to Branscombe, and inquired the distance.

'Branscombe – are you going there? Oh, I wonder what you will think of Branscombe!' she exclaimed, her white cheeks flushing, her innocent eyes sparkling with excitement.

What was Branscombe to her, I returned with indifference; and what did it matter what any stranger thought of it?

'But it is my home!' she answered, looking hurt at my careless words. 'I was born there, and married there, and have always lived at Branscombe with my people until my husband got work in this place; then we had to leave home and come and live in this cottage.'

And as I began to show interest she went on to tell me that Branscombe was, oh, such a dear, queer, funny old place! That she had been to other villages and towns – Axmouth, and Seaton, and Beer, and to Salcombe Regis and Sidmouth, and once to Exeter; but never, never had she seen a place like Branscombe – not one that she liked half so well. How strange that I had never been there – had never even heard of it! People that went there sometimes laughed at it at first, because it was such a funny, tumbledown old place; but they always said afterwards that there was no sweeter spot on the earth.

Her enthusiasm was very delightful; and, when baby cried, in the excitement of talk she opened her breast and fed it before me. A pretty sight! But for the pure white, blue-veined skin she might have been taken for a woman of Spain – the most natural, perhaps the most lovable, of the daughters of earth. But all at once she remembered that I was a stranger, and with a blush turned aside and covered her fair skin. Her shame, too, like her first simple unconscious action, was natural; for we live in a cooler climate, and are accustomed to more clothing than the Spanish; and our closer covering 'has entered the soul,' as the late Professor Kitchen Parker would have said; and that which was only becoming modesty in the English woman would in the Spanish seem rank prudishness.

In the afternoon I came to a slender stream, clear and swift, running between the hills that rose, round and large and high, on either hand, like vast downs, some grassy, others wooded. This was the Branscombe, and, following it, I came to the village; then, for a short mile my way ran by a winding path with the babbling stream below me on one side, and on the other the widely separated groups and little rows of thatched cottages.

Finally, I came to the last and largest group of all, the end of the village nearest to the sea, within ten minutes' walk of the shingly beach. Here I was glad to rest. Above, on the giant downs, were stony waste places, and heather and gorse, where the rabbits live, and had for neighbours the adder, linnet, and wheatear, and the small grey titlark that soared up and dropped back to earth all day to his tinkling little tune. On the summit of the cliff I had everything I wanted and had come to seek – the wildness and freedom of untilled earth; an unobstructed prospect, hills beyond hills of malachite, stretching away along the coast into infinitude, long leagues of red sea-wall and the wide expanse and everlasting freshness of ocean. And the village itself, the little old straggling place that had so grand a setting, I quickly found that the woman in the cottage had not succeeded in giving me a false impression of her dear home. It was just such a quaint unimproved, old-world, restful place as she had painted. It was surprising to find that there were many visitors, and one wondered where they could all stow themselves. The explanation was that those who visited Branscombe knew it, and preferred its hovels to the palaces of the fashionable seaside town. No cottage was too mean to have its guest. I saw a lady push open the cracked and warped door of an old barn and go in, pulling the door to after her – it was her bed-sitting-room. I watched a party of pretty merry girls marching, single file, down a narrow path past a pig-sty, then climb up a ladder to the window of a loft at the back of a stone cottage and disappear within. It was their bedroom. The relations between the villagers and their visitors were more intimate and kind than is usual. They lived more together, and were more free and easy in company. The men were mostly farm labourers, and after their day's work they would sit out-of-doors on the ground to smoke their pipes; and where the narrow crooked little street was narrowest – at my end of the village – when two men would sit opposite each other, each at his own door, with legs stretched out before them, their boots would very nearly touch in the middle of the road. When walking one had to step over their legs; or, if socially inclined, one could stand by and join in the conversation. When daylight faded the village was very dark – no lamp for the visitors – and very silent, only the low murmur of the sea on the shingle was audible, and the gurgling sound of a swift streamlet flowing from the hill above and hurrying through the village to mingle with the Branscombe lower down in the meadows. Such a profound darkness and quiet one expects in an inland agricultural village; here, where there were visitors from many distant towns, it was novel and infinitely refreshing.

No sooner was it dark than all were in bed and asleep; not one square path of yellow light was visible. To enjoy the sensation I went out and sat down, and listened alone to the liquid rippling, warbling sound of the swift-flowing streamlet – that sweet low music of running water to which the reed-warbler had listened thousands of years ago, striving to imitate it, until his running rippling song was perfect.

A fresh surprise and pleasure awaited me when I explored the coast east of the village; it was bold and precipitous in places, and from the summit of the cliff a very fine view of the coast-line on either hand could be obtained. Best of all, the face of the cliff itself was the breeding-place of some hundreds of herring-gulls. The eggs at the period of my visit were not yet hatched, but highly incubated, and at that stage both parents are almost constantly at home, as if in a state of anxious suspense. I had seen a good many colonies of this gull before at various breeding stations on the coast – south, west, and east – but never in conditions so singularly favourable as at this spot. From the vale where the Branscombe pours its clear waters through rough masses of shingle into the sea the ground to the east rises steeply to a height of nearly five hundred feet; the cliff is thus not nearly so high as many another, but it has features of peculiar interest. Here, in some former time, there has been a landslip, a large portion of the cliff at its highest part falling below and forming a sloping mass a chalky soil mingled with huge fragments of rock, which lies like a buttress against the vertical precipice and seems to lend it support. The fall must have occurred a very long time back, as the vegetation that overspreads the rude slope – hawthorn, furze, and ivy – has an ancient look. Here are huge masses of rock standing isolated, that resemble in their forms ruined castles, towers, and churches, some of them completely overgrown with ivy. On this rough slope, under the shelter of the cliff, with the sea at its feet, the villagers have formed their cultivated patches. The patches, wildly irregular in form, some on such steeply sloping ground as to suggest the idea that they must have been cultivated on all fours, are divided from each other by ridges and by masses of rock, deep fissures in the earth, strips of bramble and thorn and furze bushes. Altogether the effect was very singular; the huge rough mass of jumbled rock and soil, the ruin wrought by Nature in one of her Cromwellian moods, and, scattered irregularly about its surface, the plots or patches of cultivated smoothness – potato rows, green parallel lines ruled on a grey ground, and big, blue-green, equidistant cabbage-globes – each plot with its fringe of spike-like onion leaves, crinkled parsley, and other garden herbs. Here the villagers came by a narrow, steep, and difficult path they had made, to dig in their plots; while, overhead, the gulls, careless of their presence, pass and repass wholly occupied with their own affairs.

I spent hours of rare happiness at this spot in watching the birds. I could not have seen and heard them to such advantage if their breeding-place had been shared with other species. Here the herring-gulls had the rock to themselves, and looked their best in their foam-white and pearl-grey plumage and yellow legs and beaks. While I watched them they watched me; not gathered in groups, but singly or in pairs, scattered up and down all over the face of the precipice above me, perched on ledges and on jutting pieces of rock. Standing motionless thus, beautiful in form and colour, they looked like sculptured figures of gulls, set up on the projections against the rough dark wall of rock, just as sculptured figures of angels and saintly men and women are placed in niches on a cathedral front. At first they appeared quite indifferent to my presence, although in some instances near enough for their yellow irides to be visible. While unalarmed they were very silent, standing in that clear sunshine that gave their whiteness something of a crystalline appearance; or flying to and fro along the face of the cliff, purely for the delight of bathing in the warm lucent air. Gradually a change came over them. One by one those that were on the wing dropped on to some projection, until they had all settled down, and, letting my eyes range up and down over the huge wall of rock, it was plain to see that all the birds were watching me. They had made the discovery that I was a stranger. In my rough old travel-stained clothes and tweed hat I might have passed for a Branscombe villager, but I did no hoeing and digging in one of the cultivated patches; and when I deliberately sat down on a rock to watch them, they noticed it and became suspicious; and as time went on and I still remained immovable, with my eyes fixed on them, the suspicion and anxiety increased and turned to fear; and those that were sitting on their nests got up and came close to the edge of the rock, to gaze with the others and join in the loud chorus of alarm. It was a wonderful sound. Not like the tempest of noise that may be heard at the breeding-season at Lundy Island, and at many other stations where birds of several species mix their various voices – the yammeris and the yowlis, and skrykking, screeking, skrymming scowlis, and meickle noyis and shoutis, of old Dunbar's wonderful onomatopoetic lines. Here there was only one species, with a clear resonant cry, and as every bird uttered that one cry, and no other, a totally different effect was produced. The herring-gull and lesser black-backed gull resemble each other in language as they do in general appearance; both have very powerful and clear voices unlike the guttural black-headed and common gull. But the herring-gull has a shriller, more piercing voice, and resembles the black-backed species just as, in human voices, a boy's clear treble resembles a baritone. Both birds have a variety of notes; and both, when the nest is threatened with danger, utter one powerful importunate cry, which is repeated incessantly until the danger is over. And as the birds breed in communities, often very populous, and all clamour together, the effect of so many powerful and unisonant voices is very grand; but it differs in the two species, owing to the quality of their voices being different; the storm of sound produced by the black-backs is deep and solemn, while that of the herring-gulls has a ringing sharpness almost metallic.

It is probable that in the case I am describing the effect of sharpness and resonance was heightened by the position of the birds, perched motionless, scattered about on the face of the perpendicular wall of rock, all with their beaks turned in my direction, raining their cries upon me. It was not a monotonous storm of cries, but rose and fell; for after two or three minutes the excitement would abate somewhat and the cries grow fewer and fewer; then the infection would spread again, bird after bird joining the outcry; and after a while there would be another lull, and so on, wave following wave of sound. I could have spent hours, and the hours would have seemed like minutes, listening to that strange chorus of ringing chiming cries, so novel was its effect, and unlike that of any other tempest of sound produced by birds which I had ever heard.

When by way of a parting caress and benediction (given and received) I dipped my hands in Branscombe's clear streamlet it was with a feeling of tender regret that was almost a pain. For who does not make a little inward moan, an Eve's Lamentation, an unworded, 'Must I leave thee, Paradise?' on quitting any such sweet restful spot, however brief his stay in it may have been? But when I had climbed to the summit of the great down on the east side of the valley and looked on the wide land and wider sea flashed with the early sunlight I rejoiced full of glory at my freedom. For invariably when the peculiar character and charm of a place steals over and takes possession of me I begin to fear it, knowing from long experience that it will be a painful wrench to get away and that get away sooner or later I must. Now I was free once more, a wanderer with no ties, no business to transact in any town, no worries to make me miserable like others, nothing to gain and nothing to lose.

Pausing on the summit to consider which way I should go, inland, towards Axminister, or along the coast by Beer, Seton, Axmouth, and so on to Lyme Regis, I turned to have a last look and say a last good-bye to Branscombe and could hardly help waving my hand to it.

Why, I asked myself, am I not a poet, or verse-maker, so as to say my farewell in numbers? My answer was, Because I am too much occupied in seeing. There is no room and time for 'tranquillity,' since I want to go on to see something else. As Blake has it: 'Natural objects always did and do, weaken, deaden and obliterate imagination in me.'

We know however that they didn't quite quench it in him.

CHAPTER NINETEEN

Abbotsbury

Abbotsbury is an old unspoilt village, not on but near the sea, divided from it by half a mile of meadowland where all sorts of meadow and water plants flourish, and where there are extensive reed and osier beds, the roosting-place in autumn and winter of innumerable starlings. I am always delighted to come on one of these places where starlings congregate, to watch them coming in at day's decline and listen to their marvellous hubbub, and finally to see their aerial evolutions when they rise and break up in great bodies and play at clouds in the sky. When the people of the place, the squire and keepers and others who have an interest in the reeds and osiers, fall to abusing them on account of the damage they do, I put my fingers in my ears. But at Abbotsbury I did not do so, but listened with keen pleasure to the curses they vented and the story they told. This was that when the owner of Abbotsbury came down for the October shooting and found the starlings more numerous than ever, he put himself into a fine passion and reproached his keepers and other servants for not having got rid of the birds as he had desired them to do. Some of them ventured to say that it was easier said than done, whereupon the great man swore that he would do it himself without assistance from anyone, and getting out a big duck-gun he proceeded to load it with the smallest shot and went down to the reed bed and concealed himself among the bushes at a suitable distance. The birds were pouring in, and when it was growing dark and they had settled down for the night he fired his big piece into the thick of the crowd, and by and by when the birds after wheeling about for a minute or two settled down again in the same place he fired again. Then he went home, and early next morning men and boys went into the reeds and gathered a bushel or so of dead starlings. But the birds returned in their thousands that evening, and his heart being still hot against them he went out a second time to slaughter them wholesale with his big gun. Then when he had blazed into the crowd once more, and the dead and wounded fell like rain into the water below, the revulsion came and he was mad with himself for having done such a thing, and on his return to the house, or palace, he angrily told his people to 'let the starlings alone' for the future – never to molest them again!

I thought it one of the loveliest stories I had ever heard; there is no hardness comparable to that of the sportsman, yet here was one, a very monarch among them, who turned sick at his own barbarity and repented.

Beyond the flowery wet meadows, favoured by starlings and a breeding-place of swans, is the famous Chesil Bank, one of the seven wonders of Britain. And thanks to this great bank, a screen between sea and land extending about fourteen miles eastward from Portland, this part of the coast must remain inviolate from the speculative builder of seaside holiday resorts or towns of lodging-houses.

Every one has heard of the Fleet in connection with the famous swannery of Abbotsbury, the largest in the land. I had heard so much about the swannery that it had but little interest for me. The only thing about it which specially attracted my attention was seeing a swan rise up and after passing over my head as I stood on the bank fly straight out over the sea. I watched him until he had diminished to a small white spot above the horizon, and then still flying he faded from sight. Do these swans that fly away over the sea, and others which appear in small flocks or pairs at Poole Harbour and at other places on the coast, ever return to the Fleet? Probably some do, but I fancy some of these explorers must settle down in waters far from home, to return no more.

The village itself, looked upon from this same elevation, is very attractive. Life seems quieter, more peaceful there out of sight of the ocean's turbulence, out of hearing of its 'accents disconsolate.' The cottages are seen ranged in a double line along the narrow crooked street, like a procession of cows with a few laggards scattered behind the main body. One is impressed by its ancient character. The cottages are old, stone-built and thatched; older still is the church with its grey square tower, and all about are scattered the memorials of antiquity – the chantry on the hill, standing conspicuous alone, apart, above the world; the vast old abbey barn, and rough thick stone walls, ivy-draped and crowned with beautiful valerian, and other fragments that were once parts of a great religious house.

Looking back at the great round hill from the village it is impossible not to notice the intense red colour of the road that winds over its green slope. One sometimes sees on a hillside a ploughed field of red earth which at a distance might easily be taken for a field of blossoming trifolium. Viewed nearer the crimson of the clover and red of the earth are very dissimilar; distance appears to intensify the red of the soil and to soften that of the flower until they are very nearly of the same hue. The road at Abbotsbury was near and looked to me more intensely red than any ordinary red earth, and the sight was strangely pleasing. These two complementary colours, red and green, delight us most when seen thus – a little red to a good deal of green, and the more luminous the red and vivid the green the better they please us. We see this in flowers – in the red geranium, for example – where there is no brown soil below, but green of turf or herbage. I sometimes think the red campions and ragged-robins are our most beautiful wild flowers when the sun shines level on the meadow and they are like crimson flowers among the tall translucent grasses. I remember the joy it was in boyhood in early spring when the flowers were beginning to bloom, when in our gallops over the level grass pampas we came upon a patch of scarlet verbenas. The first sight of the intense blooms scattered all about the turf would make us wild with delight, and throwing ourselves from our ponies we would go down among the flowers to feast on the sight.

Green is universal, but the red earth which looks so pleasing amid the green is distributed very partially, and it may be the redness of the soil and the cliffs in Devon have given that county a more vivid personality, so to speak, than most others. Think of Kent with its white cliffs, chalk downs, and dull-coloured clays in this connection!

The humble subterraneous mole proves himself on occasions a good colourist when he finds a soil of the proper hue to burrow in, and the hillocks he throws up from numberless irregular splashes of bright red colour on a green sward. The wild animals that strike us as most beautiful, when seen against a green background, are those which bear the reddest fur – fox, squirrel, and red deer. One day, in a meadow a few miles from Abbotsbury, I came upon a herd of about fifty milch cows scattered over a considerable space of ground, some lying down, others standing ruminating, and still others moving about and cropping the long flowery grasses. All were of that fine rich red colour frequently seen in Dorset and Devon cattle, which is brighter than the reds of other red animals in this country, wild and domestic, with the sole exception of a rare variety of the collie dog. The Irish setter and red chouchou come near it. So beautiful did these red cows look in the meadow that I stood still for half an hour feasting my eyes on the sight.

No less was the pleasure I experienced when I caught sight of that road winding over the hill above the village. On going to it I found that it had looked as red as rust simply because it *was* rustearth made rich and beautiful in colour with iron, its red hue variegated with veins and streaks of deep purple or violet. I was told that there were hundreds of acres of this earth all round the place – earth so rich in iron that many a man's mouth had watered at the sight of it; also that every effort had been made to induce the owner of Abbotsbury to allow this rich mine to be worked. But, wonderful to relate, he had not been persuaded.

A hard fragment of the red stuff, measuring a couple of inches across and weighing about three ounces avoirdupois, rust-red in colour with purple streaks and yellow mottlings, is now lying before me. The mineralogist would tell me that its commercial value is naught, or something infinitesimal; which is doubtless true enough, as tens of thousands of tons of the same material lie close to the surface under the green turf and golden blossoming furze at the spot where I picked up my specimen. The lapidary would not look at it; nevertheless, it is the only article of jewellery I possess, and I value it accordingly. And I intend to keep this native ruby by me for as long as the lords of Abbotsbury continue in their present mind. The time may come when I shall be obliged to throw it away. That any millionaire should hesitate for a moment to blast and blacken any part of the earth's surface, howsoever green and refreshing to the heart it may be, when by so doing he might add to his income, seems like a fable, or a tale of fairyland. It is as if one had accidentally discovered the existence of a little fantastic realm, a survival from a remote past, almost at one's doors; a small independent province, untouched by progress, asking to be conquered and its antediluvian constitution taken from it.

From the summit of that commanding hill, over which the red path winds, a noble view presents itself of the Chesil Bank, or of about ten miles of it, running straight as any Roman road, to end beneath the rugged stupendous cliffs of Portland. The ocean itself, and not conquering Rome, raised this artificial-looking wall or rampart to stay its own proud waves. Formed of polished stones and pebbles, about two hundred yards in width, flat-topped, with steeply sloping sides, at this distance it has the appearance of a narrow yellow road or causeway between the open sea on one hand and the waters of the Fleet, a narrow lake ten miles long, on the other.

When the mackerel visit the coast, and come near enough to be taken in a draw-net, every villager who owns a share (usually a tenth) in a fishing-boat throws down his spade or whatever implement he happens to have in his hand at the moment, and hurries away to the beach to take his share in the fascinating task. At four o'clock one morning a youth, who had been down to the sea to watch, came running into the village uttering loud cries which were like excited yells – a sound to rouse the deepest sleeper. The mackerel had come! For the rest of the day there was a pretty kind of straggling procession of those who went and came between the beach and the village – men in blue cotton shirts, blue jerseys, blue jackets, and women in grey gowns and big white sun-bonnets. During the latter part of the day the proceedings were peculiarly interesting to me, a looker-on with no share in any one of the boats, owing to the catches being composed chiefly of jelly-fish. Some sympathy was felt for the toilers who strained their muscles again and again only to be mocked in the end; still, a draught of jelly-fish was more to my taste than one of mackerel. The great weight of a catch of this kind when the net was full was almost too much for the ten or twelve men engaged in drawing it up; then (to the sound of deep curses from those of the men who were not religious) the net would be opened and the great crystalline hemispheres, hyaline blue and delicate salmon-pink in colour, would slide back into the water. Such rare and exquisite colours have these great glassy flowers of ocean that to see them was a feast; and every time a net was hauled up my prayer – which I was careful not to repeat aloud – was, Heaven send another big draught of jelly-fish!

The sun, sinking over the hills towards Swyre and Bridport, turned crimson before it touched the horizon. The sky became luminous; the yellow Chesil Bank, stretching long leagues away, and the hills behind it, changed their colours to violet. The rough sea near the beach glittered like gold; the deep green water, flecked with foam, was mingled with fire; the one boat that remained on it, tossing up and down near the beach, was like a boat of ebony in a glittering fiery sea. A dozen men were drawing up the last net; but when they gathered round to see what they had taken – mackerel or jelly-fish – I cared no longer to look with them. That sudden, wonderful glory which had fallen on the earth and sea had smitten me as well and changed me; and I was like some needy homeless tramp who has found a shilling piece, and, even while he is gloating over it, all at once sees a great treasure before him – glittering gold in heaps, and all rarest sparkling gems, more than he can gather up.

But it is a poor simile. No treasures in gold and gems, though heaped waist-high all about, could produce in the greediest man, hungry for earthly pleasures, a delight, a rapture, equal to mine. For this joy was of another and higher order and very rare, and was a sense of lightness and freedom from all trammels as if the body had become air, essence, energy, or soul, and of union with all visible nature, one with sea and land and the entire vast overarching sky.

We read of certain saints who were subject to experiences of this kind that they were 'snatched up' into some supramundane region, and that they stated on their return to earth that it was not lawful for them to speak of the things they had witnessed. The humble naturalist and nature-worshipper can only witness the world glorified – transfigured; what he finds is the important thing. I fancy the mystics would have been nearer the mark if they had said that their experiences during their period of exaltation could not be reported, or that it would be idle to report them, since their questioners lived on the ground and would be quite incapable on account of the mind's limitations of conceiving a state above it and outside of its own experience.

The glory passed and with it the exaltation: the earth and sea turned grey; the last boat was drawn up on the slope and the men departed slowly: only one remained, a rough-looking youth, about fifteen years old. Some important matter which he was revolving in his mind had detained him alone on the darkening beach. He sat down, then stood up and gazed at the rolling wave after wave to roar and hiss on the shingle at his feet; then he moved restlessly about, crunching pebbles beneath his thick boots; finally, making up his mind, he took off his coat, threw it down, and rolled up his shirt-sleeves, with the resolute air of a man about to engage in a fight with an adversary nearly as big as himself. Stepping back a little space, he made a rush at the sea, not to cast himself in it, but only, as it turned out, with the object of catching some water in the hollow of his hands from the top of an incoming wave. He only succeeded in getting his legs wet, and in hastily retreating he fell on his back. Nothing daunted, he got up and renewed the assault, and when he succeeded in catching water in his hands he dashed it on and vigorously rubbed it over his dirty face. After repeating the operation about a dozen times, receiving meanwhile several falls and wettings, he appeared satisfied, put on his coat and marched away homewards with a composed air.

CHAPTER TWENTY

Salisbury Revisited

Since that visit to Salisbury, described in a former chapter, when I watched and listened to the doves in those cold days in early spring, I have been there a good many times, but never at the time when the bird colony is most interesting to observe, just before and during the early part of the breeding-season. At length, in the early days of June, 1908, the wished opportunity was mine – wished yet feared, seeing that it was possible some disaster had fallen upon that unique colony of stock-doves. It is true they appeared to be long established and well able to maintain their foothold on the building in spite of malicious persecuting daws, but there was nothing to show that they had been long there, seeing that it had been observed by no person but myself that the cathedral doves were stock-doves and not the domestic pigeon found on other large buildings. Great was my happiness to find them still there, as well as the daws and all the other feathered people who make this great building their home; even the kestrels were not wanting. There were three there one morning, quarrelling with the daws in the old way in the old place, halfway up the soaring spire. The doves were somewhat diminished in number, but there were a good many pairs still, and I found no dead young ones lying about, as they were now probably grown too large to be ejected, but several young daws, about a dozen I think, fell to the ground during my stay. Undoubtedly they were dragged out of their nests and thrown down, perhaps by daws at enmity with their parents, or it may be by the doves, who are not meek-spirited, as we have seen, or they would not be where they are, and may on occasion retaliate by invading their black enemies' nesting-holes.

Swallows, martins, and swifts were numerous, the martins especially, and it was beautiful to see them for ever wheeling about in a loose swarm about the building. They reminded me of bees and flies, and sometimes with a strong light on them they were like those small polished black and silvery-white beetles (*Gyrinus*) which we see in companies on the surface of pools and streams, perpetually gliding and whirling about in a sort of complicated dance. They looked very small at a height of a couple of hundred feet from the ground, and their smallness and numbers and lively and eccentric motions made them very insect-like.

The starlings and sparrows were in a small minority among the breeders, but including these there were seven species in all, and as far as I could make out numbered about three hundred and fifty birds – probably the largest wild bird colony on any building in England.

Nor could birds in all this land find a more beautiful building to nest on, unless I except Wells Cathedral solely on account of its west front, beloved of daws, and where their numerous black company have so fine an appearance. Wells has its west front; Salisbury, so vast in size, is yet a marvel of beauty in its entirety; and seeing it as I now did every day and wanting nothing better, I wondered at my want of enthusiasm on a previous visit. Still, to me, the bird company, the sight of their airy gambols and their various voices, from the deep human-like dove tone to the perpetual subdued rippling, running-water sound of the aerial martins, must always be a principal element in the beautiful effect. Nor do I know a building where Nature has done more in enhancing the loveliness of man's work with her added colouring. The way too in which the colours are distributed is an example of Nature's most perfect artistry; on the lower, heavier buttressed parts, where the darkest hues should be, we find the browns and rust-reds of the minute aerial alga, mixed with the greys of lichen, these darker stainings extending upwards to a height of fifty or sixty feet, in places higher, then giving place to more delicate hues, the pale tender greens and greenish greys, in places tinged with yellow, the colours always appearing brightest on the smooth surface between the windows and sculptured parts. The effect depends a good deal on atmosphere and weather: on a day of flying clouds and a blue sky, with a brilliant sunshine on the vast building after a shower, the colouring is most beautiful. It varies more than in the case of colour in the material itself or of pigments, because it is a 'living' colour, as Crabbe rightly says in his lumbering verse:

> The living stains, which Nature's hand alone,
> Profuse of life, pours out upon the stone.

Greys, greens, yellows, and browns and rust-reds are but the colours of a variety of lowly vegetable forms, mostly lichens and the aerial alga called iolithus.

Without this colouring, its 'living stains,' Salisbury would not have fascinated me as it did during this last visit. It would have left me cold though all the architects and artists had assured me that it was the most perfectly beautiful building on earth.

I also found an increasing charm in the interior, and made the discovery that I could go oftener and spend more hours in this cathedral without a sense of fatigue or depression than in any other one known to me, because it has less of that peculiar character which we look for and almost invariably find in our cathedrals. It has not the rich sombre majesty, the dim religious light and heavy vault-like atmosphere of the other great fanes. So airy and light is it that it is almost like being out of doors. You do not experience that instantaneous change, as of a curtain being drawn excluding the light and air of day and of being shut in, which you have on entering other religious houses. This is due, first, to the vast size of the interior, the immense length of the nave, and the unobstructed view one has inside owing to the removal by the 'vandal' Wyatt of the old ponderous stone screen – an act for which I bless while all others curse his memory; secondly, to the comparatively small amount of stained glass there is to intercept the light. So graceful and beautiful is the interior that it can bear the light, and light suits it best, just as a twilight best suits Exeter and Winchester and other cathedrals with heavy sculptured roofs. One marvels at a building so vast in size which yet produces the effect of a palace in fairyland, or of a cathedral not built with hands but brought into existence by a miracle.

I began to think it not safe to stay in that place too long lest it should compel me to stay there always or cause me to feel dissatisfied and homesick when away.

But the interior of itself would never have won me, as I had not expected to be won by any building made by man; and from the inside I would pass out only to find a fresh charm in that part where Nature had come more to man's aid.

Walking on the cathedral green one morning, glancing from time to time at the vast building and its various delicate shades of colour, I asked myself why I kept my eyes as if on purpose away from it most of the time, now on the trees, then on the turf, and again on some one walking there – why, in fact, I allowed myself only an occasional glance at the object I was there solely to look at. I knew well enough, but had never put it into plain words for my own satisfaction.

We are all pretty familiar from experience with the limitations of the sense of smell and the fact that agreeable odours please us only fitfully; the sensation comes as a pleasing shock, a surprise, and is quickly gone. If we attempt to keep it for some time by deliberately smelling a fragrant flower or any perfume, we begin to have a sense of failure as if we had exhausted the sense, keen as it was a moment ago. There must be an interval of rest for the nerve before the sensation can be renewed in its first freshness. Now it is the same, though in a less degree, with the more important sense of sight. We look long and steadily at a thing to know it, and the longer and more fixedly we look the better, if it engages the reasoning faculties; but an aesthetic pleasure cannot be increased or retained in that way. We must look, merely glancing as it were, and look again, and then again, with intervals, receiving the image in the brain even as we receive the 'nimble emanations' of a flower, and the image is all the brighter for coming intermittently. In a large prospect we are not conscious of this limitation because of the wideness of the field and the number and variety of objects or points of interest in it; the vision roams hither and thither over it and receives a continuous stream or series of pleasing impressions; but to gaze fixedly at the most beautiful object in nature or art does but diminish the pleasure. Practically it ceases to be beautiful and only recovers the first effect after we have given the mind an interval of rest.

Strolling about the green with this thought in my mind, I began to pay attention to the movements of a man who was manifestly there with the same object as myself – to look at the cathedral. I had seen him there for quite half an hour, and now began to be amused at the emphatic manner in which he displayed his interest in the building. He walked up and down the entire length and would then back away a distance of a hundred yards from the walls and stare up at the spire, then slowly approach, still gazing up, until coming to a stop when quite near the wall he would remain with his eyes still fixed aloft, the back of his head almost resting on his back between his shoulders. His hat somehow kept on his head, but his attitude reminded me of a saying of the Arabs who, to give an idea of the height of a great rock or other tall object, say that to look up at it causes your turban to fall off. The Americans, when they were chewers of tobacco, had a different expression; they said that to look up at so tall a thing caused the tobacco juice to run down your throat.

His appearance when I approached him interested me too. His skin was the colour of old brown leather and he had a big arched nose, clear light blue very shrewd eyes, and a big fringe or hedge of ragged white beard under his chin; and he was dressed in a new suit of rough dark brown tweeds, evidently home-made. When I spoke to him, saying something about the cathedral, he joyfully responded in broadest Scotch. It was, he said, the first English cathedral he had ever seen and he had never seen anything made by man to equal it in beauty. He had come, he told me, straight from his home and birthplace, a small village in the north of Scotland, shut out from the world by great hills where the heather grew knee-deep. He had never been in England before, and had come directly to Salisbury on a visit to a relation.

'Well,' I said, 'now you have looked at it outside come in with me and see the interior.'

But he refused: it was enough for one day to see the outside of such a building: he wanted no more just then. To-morrow would be soon enough to see it inside; it would be the Sabbath and he would go and worship there.

'Are you an Anglican then?' I asked.

He replied that there were no Anglicans in *his* village. They had two churches – the Church of Scotland and the Free Church.

'And what,' said I, 'will your minister say to your going to worship in a cathedral? We have all denominations here in Salisbury, and you will perhaps find a Presbyterian place to worship in.'

'Now it's strange your saying that!' he returned, with a dry little laugh. 'I've just had a letter from him the morning and he writes on this varra subject. 'Let me advise you,' he tells me in the letter, 'to attend the service in Salisbury Cathedral. Nae doot,' he says, 'there are many things in it you'll disapprove of, but not everything perhaps, and I'd like ye to go.''

I was a little sorry for him next day when we had an ordination service, very long, complicated, and, I should imagine, exceedingly difficult to follow by a wild Presbyterian from the hills. He probably disapproved of most of it, but I greatly admired him for refusing to see anything more of the cathedral than the outside on the first day. His method was better than that of an American (from Indiana, he told me) I met the following day at the hotel. He gave two hours and a half, including attendance at the morning service, to the cathedral, inside and out, then rushed off for an hour at Stonehenge, fourteen miles away, on a hired bicycle. I advised him to take another day – I did not want to frighten him by saying a week – and he replied that that would make him miss Winchester. After cycling back from Stonehenge he would catch a train to Winchester and get there in time to have some minutes in the cathedral before the doors closed. He was due in London next morning. He had already missed Durham Cathedral in the north through getting interested in and wasting too much time over some place when he was going there. Again, he had missed Exeter Cathedral in the south, and it would be a little too bad to miss Winchester too!

CHAPTER TWENTY-ONE

Stonehenge

That American from Indiana! As it was market day at Salisbury I asked him before we parted if he had seen the market, also if they had market days in the country towns in his State? He said he had looked in at the market on his way back from the cathedral. No, they had nothing of the kind in his State. Indiana was covered with a network of railroads and electric tram lines, and all country produce, down to the last new-laid egg, was collected and sent off and conveyed each morning to the towns, where it was always market day.

How sad! thought I. Poor Indiana, that once had wildness and romance and memories of a vanished race, and has now only its pretty meaningless name!

'I suppose,' he said, before getting on his bicycle, 'there's nothing beside the cathedral and Stonehenge to see in Wiltshire?'

'No, nothing,' I returned, 'and you'll think the time wasted in seeing Stonehenge.'

'Why?'

'Only a few old stones to see.'

But he went, and I have no doubt did think the time wasted, but it would be some consolation to him, on the other side, to be able to say that he had seen it with his own eyes.

How did these same 'few old stones' strike *me* on a first visit? It was one of the greatest disillusionments I ever experienced. Stonehenge looked small – pitiably small! For it is a fact that mere size is very much to us, in spite of all the teachings of science. We have heard of Stonehenge in our childhood or boyhood – that great building of unknown origin and antiquity, its circles of stones, some still standing, others lying prostrate, like the stupendous half-shattered skeleton of a giant or monster whose stature reached to the clouds. It stands, we read or were told, on Salisbury Plain. To my uninformed, childish mind a plain anywhere was like the plain on which I was born – an absolutely level area stretching away on all sides into infinitude; and although the effect is of a great extent of earth, we know that we actually see very little of it, that standing on a level plain we have a very near horizon. On this account any large object appearing on it, such as a horse or tree or a big animal, looks very much bigger than it would on land with a broken surface.

Oddly enough, my impossible Stonehenge was derived from a sober description and an accompanying plate in a sober work – a gigantic folio in two volumes entitled A New System of Geography, dated some time in the eighteenth century. How this ponderous work ever came to be out on the pampas, over six thousand miles from the land of its origin, is a thing to wonder at. I remember that the Stonehenge plate greatly impressed me and that I sacrilegiously cut it out of the book so as to have it!

Now we know, our reason tells us continually, that the mental pictures formed in childhood are false because the child and man have different standards, and furthermore the child mind exaggerates everything; nevertheless, such pictures persist until the scene or object so visualized is actually looked upon and the old image shattered. This refers to scenes visualized with the inner eye, but the disillusion is almost as great when we return to a home left in childhood or boyhood and look on it once more with the man's eyes. How small it is! How diminished the hills, and the trees that grew to such a vast height, whose tops once seemed 'so close against the sky' – what poor little trees they now are! And the house itself, how low it is; and the rooms that seemed so wide and lofty, where our footfalls and childish voices sounded as in some vast hall, how little and how mean they look!

Children, they are very little,

the poet says, and they measure things by their size; but it seems odd that unless we grow up amid the scenes where our first impressions were received they should remain unaltered in the adult mind. The most amusing instance of a false picture of something seen in childhood and continuing through life I have met was that of an Italian peasant I knew in South America. He liked to talk to me about the cranes, those great and wonderful birds he had become acquainted with in childhood in his home on the plains of Lombardy. The birds, of course, only appeared in autumn and spring when migrating, and passed over at a vast height above the earth. These birds, he said, were so big and had such great wings that if they came down on the flat earth they would be incapable of rising, hence they only alighted on the tops of high mountains, and as there was nothing for them to eat in such places, it being naked rock and ice, they were compelled to subsist on each other's droppings. Now it came to pass that one year during his childhood a crane, owing to some accident, came down to the ground near his home. The whole population of the village turned out to see so wonderful a bird, and were amazed at its size; it was, he said, the strangest sight he had ever looked on. How big was it? I asked him; was it as big as an ostrich? An ostrich, he said, was nothing to it; I might as well ask him how it compared with a lapwing. He could give me no measurements: it happened when he was a child; he had forgotten the exact size, but he had seen it with his own eyes and he could see it now in his mind – the biggest bird in the world. Very well, I said, if he could see it plainly in his mind he could give some rough idea of the wing-spread – how much would it measure from tip to tip? He said it was perhaps fifty yards – perhaps a good deal more!

A similar trick was played by my mind about Stonehenge. As a child I had stood in imagination before it, gazing up awestruck on those stupendous stones or climbing and crawling like a small beetle on them. And what at last did I see with my physical eyes? Walking over the downs, miscalled a plain, anticipating something tremendous, I finally got away from the woods at Amesbury and spied the thing I sought before me far away on the slope of a green down, and stood still and then sat down in pure astonishment. Was *this* Stonehenge – this cluster of poor little grey stones, looking in the distance like a small flock of sheep or goats grazing on that immense down! How incredibly insignificant it appeared to me, dwarfed by its surroundings – woods and groves and farmhouses, and by the vast extent of rolling down country visible at that point. It was only when I had recovered from the first shock, when I had got to the very place and stood among the stones, that I began to experience something of the feeling appropriate to the occasion.

The feeling, however, must have been very slight, since it permitted me to become interested in the appearance and actions of a few sparrows inhabiting the temple. The common sparrow is parasitical on man, consequently but rarely found at any distance from human habitations, and it seemed a little strange to find them at home at Stonehenge on the open plain. They were very active, carrying up straws and feathers to the crevices on the trioliths where the massive imposts rest on the upright stones. I noticed the birds because of their bright appearance: they were lighter coloured than any sparrows I have ever seen, and one cock bird when flying to and fro in the sunlight looked almost white. I formed the idea that this small colony of about a dozen birds had been long established at that place, and that the change in their colouring was a direct result of the unusual conditions in which they existed, where there was no shade and shelter of trees and bushes, and they were perpetually exposed for generations to the full light of the wide open sky.

On revisiting Stonehenge after an interval of some years I looked for my sparrows and failed to find them. It was at the breeding-season, when they would have been there had they still existed. No doubt the little colony had been extirpated by a sparrow-hawk or by the human guardians of 'The Stones,' as the temple is called by the natives.

It remains to tell of my latest visit to 'The Stones.' I had resolved to go once in my life with the current or crowd to see the sun rise on the morning of the longest day at that place. This custom or fashion is a declining one: ten or twelve years ago, as many as one or two thousand persons would assemble during the night to wait the great event, but the watchers have now diminished to a few hundreds, and on some years to a few scores. The fashion, no doubt, had its origin when Sir Norman Lockyer's theories, about Stonehenge as a Sun Temple placed so that the first rays of sun on the longest day of the year should fall on the centre of the so-called altar or sacrificial stone placed in the middle of the circle, began to be noised about the country, and accepted by every one as the true reading of an ancient riddle. But I gather from natives in the district that it is an old custom for people to go and watch for sunrise on the morning of June 21. A dozen or a score of natives, mostly old shepherds and labourers who lived near, would go and sit there for a few hours and after sunrise would trudge home, but whether or not there is any tradition or belief associated with the custom I have not ascertained. 'How long has the custom existed?' I asked a field labourer. 'From the time of the old people – the Druids,' he answered, and I gave it up.

To be near the spot I went to stay at Shrewton, a downland village four miles from 'The Stones'; or rather a group of five pretty little villages, almost touching but distinct, like five flowers or five berries on a single stem, each with its own old church and individual or parish life. It is a pretty tree-shaded place, full of the crooning sound of turtle-doves, hidden among the wide silent open downs and watered by a clear swift stream, or winter bourne, which dries up during the heats of late summer, and flows again after the autumn rains, 'when the springs rise' in the chalk hills. While here, I rambled on the downs and haunted 'The Stones.' The road from Shrewton to Amesbury, a straight white band lying across a green country, passes within a few yards of Stonehenge: on the right side of this narrow line the land is all private property, but on the left side and as far as one can see it mostly belongs to the War Office and is dotted over with camps. I roamed about freely enough on both sides, sometimes spending hours at a stretch, not only on Government land but 'within bounds,' for the pleasure of spying on the military from a hiding-place in some pine grove or furze patch. I was seldom challenged, and the sentinels I came across were very mild-mannered men; they never ordered me away; they only said, or hinted, that the place I was in was not supposed to be free to the public.

I come across many persons who lament the recent great change on Salisbury Plain. It is hateful to them; the sight of the camp and troops marching and drilling, of men in khaki scattered about everywhere over a hundred square leagues of plain; the smoke of firing and everlasting booming of guns. It is a desecration; the wild ancient charm of the land has been destroyed in their case, and it saddens and angers them. I was pretty free from these uncomfortable feelings.

It is said that one of the notions the Japanese have about the fox – a semi-sacred animal with them – is that, if you chance to see one crossing your path in the morning, all that comes before your vision on that day will be illusion. As an illustration of this belief it is related that a Japanese who witnessed the eruption of Krakatoa, when the heavens were covered with blackness and kindled with intermitting flashes and the earth shaken by the detonations, and when all others, thinking the end of the world had come, were swooning with extreme fear, viewed it without a tremor as a very sublime but illusory spectacle. For on that very morning he had seen a fox cross his path.

A somewhat similar effect is produced on our minds if we have what may be called a sense of historical time – a consciousness of the transitoriness of most things human – if we see institutions and works as the branches on a pine or larch, which fail and die and fall away successively while the tree itself lives for ever, and if we measure their duration not by our own few swift years, but by the life of nations and races of men. It is, I imagine, a sense capable of cultivation, and enables us to look upon many of man's doings that would otherwise vex and pain us, and, as some say, destroy all the pleasure of our lives, not exactly as an illusion, as if we were Japanese and had seen a fox in the morning, but at all events in what we call a philosophic spirit.

What troubled me most was the consideration of the effect of the new conditions on the wild life of the plain – or of a very large portion of it. I knew of this before, but it was nevertheless exceedingly unpleasant when I came to witness it myself when I took to spying on the military as an amusement during my idle time. Here we have tens of thousands of very young men, boys in mind, the best fed, healthiest, happiest crowd of boys in all the land, living in a pure bracing atmosphere, far removed from towns, and their amusements and temptations, all mad for pleasure and excitement of some kind to fill their vacant hours each day and their holidays. Naturally they take to birds'-nesting and to hunting every living thing they encounter during their walks on the downs. Every wild thing runs and flies from them, and is chased or stoned, the weak-winged young are captured, and the nests picked or kicked up out of the turf. In this way the creatures are being extirpated, and one can foresee that when hares and rabbits are no more, and even the small birds of the plain, larks, pipits, wheatears, stonechats, and whincats, have vanished, the hunters in khaki will take to the chase of yet smaller creatures – crane-flies and butterflies and dragon-flies, and even the fantastic, elusive hover-flies which the hunters of little game will perhaps think the most entertaining fly of all.

But it would be idle to grieve much at this small incidental and inevitable result of making use of the plain as a military camp and training-ground. The old god of war is not yet dead and rotting on his iron hills; he is on the chalk hills with us just now, walking on the elastic turf, and one is glad to mark in his brown skin and sparkling eyes how thoroughly alive he is.

A little after midnight on the morning of June 21, 1908, a Shrewton cock began to crow, and that trumpet sound, which I never hear without a stirring of the blood, on account of old associations, informed me that the late moon had risen or was about to rise, linking the midsummer evening and morning twilights, and I set off to Stonehenge. It was a fine still night, without a cloud in the pale, dusky blue sky, thinly sprinkled with stars, and the crescent moon coming up above the horizon. After the cock ceased crowing a tawny owl began to hoot, and the long tremulous mellow sound followed me for some distance from the village, and then there was perfect silence, broken occasionally by the tinkling bells of a little company of cyclists speeding past towards 'The Stones.' I was in no hurry: I only wished I had started sooner to enjoy Salisbury Plain at its best time, when all the things which offend the lover of nature are invisible and non-existent. Later, when the first light began to appear in the east before two o'clock, it was no false dawn, but insensibly grew brighter and spread further, until touches of colour, very delicate, palest amber, then tender yellow and rose and purple, began to show. I felt then as we invariably feel on such occasions, when some special motive has called us forth in time to witness this heavenly change, as of a new creation –

> The miracle of diuturnity
> Whose instancy unbeds the lark,

that all the days of my life on which I had not witnessed it were wasted days!

O that unbedding of the lark! The world that was so still before now all at once had a sound; not a single song and not in one place, but a sound composed of a thousand individual sounds, rising out of the dark earth at a distance on my right hand and up into the dusky sky, spreading far and wide even as the light was spreading on the opposite side of the heavens – a sound as of multitudinous twanging, girding, and clashing instruments, mingled with shrill piercing voices that were not like the voices of earthly beings. They were not human nor angelic, but passionless, and it was as if the whole visible world, the dim grassy plain and the vast pale sky sprinkled with paling stars, moonlit and dawnlit, had found a voice to express the mystery and glory of the morning.

It was but eight minutes past two o'clock when this 'unbedding of the lark' began, and the heavenly music lasted about fourteen minutes, then died down to silence, to recommence about half an hour later. At first I wondered why the sound was at a distance from the road on my right hand and not on my left hand as well. Then I remembered what I had seen on that side, how the 'boys' at play on Sundays and in fact every day hunt the birds and pull their nests out, and I could only conclude that the lark has been pretty well wiped out from all that part of the plain over which the soldiers range.

At Stonehenge I found a good number of watchers, about a couple of hundred, already assembled, but more were coming in continually, and a mile or so of the road to Amesbury visible from 'The Stones' had at times the appearance of a ribbon of fire from the lamps of this continuous stream of coming cyclists. Altogether about five to six hundred persons gathered at 'The Stones,' mostly young men on bicycles who came from all the Wiltshire towns within easy distance, from Salisbury to Bath. I had a few good minutes at the ancient temple when the sight of the rude upright stones looking black against the moonlit and star-sprinkled sky produced an unexpected feeling in me: but the mood could not last; the crowd was too big and noisy, and the noises they made too suggestive of a Bank Holiday crowd at the Crystal Palace.

At three o'clock a ribbon of slate-grey cloud appeared above the eastern horizon, and broadened by degrees, and pretty soon made it evident that the sun would be hidden at its rising at a quarter to four. The crowd, however, was not down-hearted; it sang and shouted; and by and by, just outside the barbed-wire enclosure a rabbit was unearthed, and about three hundred young men with shrieks of excitement set about its capture. It was a lively scene, a general scrimmage, in which everyone was trying to capture an elusive football with ears and legs to it, which went darting and spinning about hither and thither among the multitudinous legs, until earth compassionately opened and swallowed poor distracted bunny up. It was but little better inside the enclosure, where the big fallen stones behind the altar-stone, in the middle, on which the first rays of sun would fall, were taken possession of by a crowd of young men who sat and stood packed together like guillemots on a rock. These too, cheated by that rising cloud of the spectacle they had come so far to see, wanted to have a little fun, and began to be very obstreperous. By and by they found out an amusement very much to their taste.

Motor-cars were now arriving every minute, bringing important-looking persons who had timed their journeys so as to come upon the scene a little before 3:45, when the sun would show on the horizon; and whenever one of these big gentlemen appeared within the circle of stones, especially if he was big physically and grotesque-looking in his motorist get-up, he was greeted with a tremendous shout. In most cases he would start back and stand still, astonished at such an outburst, and then, concluding that the only way to save his dignity was to face the music, he would step hurriedly across the green space to hide himself behind the crowd.

The most amusing case was that of a very tall person adorned with an exceedingly long, bright red beard, who had on a Glengarry cap and a great shawl over his overcoat. The instant this unfortunate person stepped into the arena a general wild cry of 'Scotland for ever!' was raised, followed by such cheers and yells that the poor man actually staggered back as if he had received a blow, then seeing there was no other way out of it, he too rushed across the open space to lose himself among the others.

All this proved very entertaining, and I was glad to laugh with the crowd, thinking that after all we were taking a very mild revenge on our hated enemies, the tyrants of the roads.

The fun over, I went soberly back to my village, and finding it impossible to get to sleep I went to Sunday-morning service at Shrewton Church. It was strangely restful there after that noisy morning crowd at Stonehenge. The church is white stone with Norman pillars and old oak beams laid over the roof painted or dis-tempered blue – a quiet, peaceful blue. There was also a good deal of pleasing blue colour in the glass of the east window. The service was, as I almost invariably find it in a village church, beautiful and impressive. Listening to the music of prayer and praise, with some natural outdoor sound to fill up the pauses – the distant crow of a cock or the song of some bird close by – a corn-bunting or wren or hedge-sparrow – and the bright sunlight filling the interior, I felt as much refreshed as if kind nature's sweet restorer, balmy sleep, had visited me that morning. The sermon was nothing to me; I scarcely heard it, but understood that it was about the Incarnation and the perfection of the plan of salvation and the unreasonableness of the Higher Criticism and of all who doubt because they do not understand. I remembered vaguely that on three successive Sundays in three village churches in the wilds of Wiltshire I had heard sermons preached on and against the Higher Criticism. I thought it would have been better in this case if the priest had chosen to preach on Stonehenge and had said that he devoutly wished we were sun-worshippers, like the Persians, as well as Christians; also that we were Buddhists, and worshippers of our dead ancestors like the Chinese, and that we were pagans and idolaters who bow down to sticks and stones, if all these added cults would serve to make us more reverent. And I wish he could have said that it was as irreligious to go to Stonehenge, that ancient temple which man raised to the unknown god thousands of years ago, to indulge in noise and horseplay at the hour of sunrise, as it would be to go to Salisbury Cathedral for such a purpose.

CHAPTER TWENTY-TWO

The Village and 'The Stones'

My experiences at 'The Stones' had left me with the idea that but for the distracting company the hours I spent there would have been very sweet and precious in spite of the cloud in the east. Why then, I asked, not go back on another morning, when I would have the whole place to myself? If a cloud did not matter much it would matter still less that it was not the day of the year when the red disc flames on the watcher's sight directly over that outstanding stone and casts first a shadow then a ray of light on the altar. In the end I did not say good-bye to the village on that day, but settled down to listen to the tales of my landlady, or rather to another instalment of her life-story and to further chapters in the domestic history of those five small villages in one. I had already been listening to her every evening, and at odd times during the day, for over a week, at first with interest, then a little impatiently. I was impatient at being kept in, so to speak. Out-of-doors the world was full of light and heat, full of sounds of wild birds and fragrance of flowers and new-mown hay; there were also delightful children and some that were anything but delightful – dirty, ragged little urchins of the slums. For even these small rustic villages have their slums; and it was now the time when the young birds were fluttering out of their nests – their hunger cries could be heard everywhere; and the ragged little barbarians were wild with excitement, chasing and stoning the flutterers to slay them; or when they succeeded in capturing one without first having broken its wings or legs it was to put it in a dirty cage in a squalid cottage to see it perish miserably in a day or two. Perhaps I succeeded in saving two or three threatened lives in the lanes and secret green places by the stream; perhaps I didn't; but in any case it was some satisfaction to have made the attempt.

Now all this made me a somewhat impatient listener to the village tales – the old unhappy things, for they were mostly old and always unhappy; yet in the end I had to listen. It was her eyes that did it. At times they had an intensity in their gaze which made them almost uncanny, something like the luminous eyes of an animal hungrily fixed on its prey. They held me, though not because they glittered: I could have gone away if I had thought proper, and remained to listen only because the meaning of that singular look in her grey-green eyes, which came into them whenever I grew restive, had dawned on my careless mind.

She was an old woman with snow-white hair, which contrasted rather strangely with her hard red colour; but her skin was smooth, her face well shaped, with fine aquiline features. No doubt it had been a very handsome face though never beautiful, I imagine; it was too strong and firm and resolute; too like the face of some man we see, which, though we have but a momentary sight of it in a passing crowd, affects us like a sudden puff of icy-cold air – the revelation of a singular and power-ful personality. Yet she was only a poor old broken-down woman in a Wiltshire village, held fast in her chair by a hopeless infirmity. With her legs paralysed she was like that prince in the Eastern tale on whom an evil spell had been cast, turning the lower half of his body into marble. But she did not, like the prince, shed incessant tears and lament her mis-erable destiny with a loud voice. She was patient and cheerful always, resigned to the will of Heaven, and – a strange thing this to record of an old woman in a village! – she would never speak of her ailments. But though powerless in body her mind was vigorous and active teeming with memories of all the vicissitudes of her exceedingly eventful, busy life, from the time when she left her village as a young girl to fight her way in the great world to her return to end her life in it, old and broken, her fight over, her children and grandchildren dead or grown up and scattered about the earth.

Chance having now put me in her way, she concluded after a few preliminary or tentative talks that she had got hold of an ideal listener; but she feared to lose me – she wanted me to go on listening for ever. That was the reason of that painfully intense hungry look in her eyes; it was because she discovered certain signs of lassitude or impatience in me, a desire to get up and go away and refresh myself in the sun and wind. Poor old woman, she could not spring upon and hold me fast when I attempted to move off, or pluck me back with her claws; she could only gaze with fiercely pleading eyes and say nothing; and so, without being fascinated, I very often sat on listening still when I would gladly have been out-of-doors.

She was a good fluent talker; moreover, she studied her listener, and finding that my interest in her own interminable story was becoming exhausted she sought for other subjects, chiefly the strange events in the lives of men and women who had lived in the village and who had long been turned to dust. They were all more or less tragical in character, and it astonished me to think that I had stayed in a dozen or twenty, perhaps forty, villages in Wiltshire, and had heard stories equally strange and moving in pretty well every one of them.

If each of these small centres possessed a scribe of genius, or at any rate one with a capacity for taking pains, who would collect and print in proper form these remembered events, every village would in time have its own little library of local history, the volumes labelled respectively, 'A Village Tragedy', 'The Fields of Dulditch', 'Life's Little Ironies', 'Children's Children', and various others whose titles every reader will be able to supply.

The effect of a long spell of listening to these unwritten tragedies was sometimes strong enough to cloud my reason, for on going directly forth into the bright sunshine and listening to the glad sounds which filled the air, it would seem that this earth was a paradise and that all creation rejoiced in everlasting happiness excepting man alone who – mysterious being! – was born to trouble and disaster as the sparks fly upwards. A pure delusion, due to our universal and ineradicable passion for romance and tragedy. Tell a man of a hundred humdrum lives which run their quiet contented course in this village, and the monotonous unmoving story, or hundred stories, will go in at one ear and out at the other. Therefore such stories are not told and not remembered. But that which stirs our pity and terror – the frustrate life, the glorious promise which was not fulfilled, the broken hearts and broken fortunes, and passion, crime, remorse, retribution – all this prints itself on the mind, and every such life is remembered for ever and passed on from generation to generation. But it would really form only one brief chapter in the long, long history of the village life with its thousand chapters.

The truth is, if we live in fairly natural healthy condition, we are just as happy as the lower animals. Some philosopher has said that the chief pleasure in a man's life, as in that of a cow, consists in the processes of mastication, deglutition, and digestion, and I am very much inclined to agree with him. The thought of death troubles us very little – we do not believe in it. A familiar instance is that of the consumptive, whose doctor and friends have given him up and wait but to see the end, while he, deluded man, still sees life, an illimitable, green, sunlit prospect, stretching away to an infinite distance before him. Death is a reality only when it is very near, so close on us that we can actually hear its swift stoaty feet rustling over the dead leaves, and for a brief bitter space we actually know that his sharp teeth will presently be in our throat.

Out in the blessed sunshine I listen to a blackcap warbling very beautifully in a thorn bush near the cottage; then to the great shout of excited joy of the children just released from school, as they rush pell-mell forth and scatter about the village, and it strikes me that the bird in the thorn is not more blithe-hearted than they. An old rook – I fancy he is old, a many-wintered crow – is loudly caw-cawing from the elm tree top; he has been abroad all day in the fields and has seen his young able to feed themselves; and his own crop full, and now he is calling to the others to come and sit there to enjoy the sunshine with him. I doubt if he is happier than the human inhabitants of the village, the field labourers and shepherds who have been out toiling since the early hours, and are now busy in their own gardens and allotments or placidly smoking their pipes at their cottage doors.

But I could not stay longer in that village of old unhappy memories and of quiet, happy, uninteresting lives that leave no memory, so after waiting two more days I forced myself to say good-bye to my poor old landlady. Or rather to say 'Good night,' as I had to start at one o'clock in the morning so as to have a couple, of hours before sunrise at 'The Stones' on my way to Salisbury. Her latest effort to detain me a day longer had been made and there was no more to say.

'Do you know,' she said in a low mysterious voice, 'that it is not safe to be alone at midnight on this long lonely road – the loneliest place in all Salisbury Plain?' 'The safest,' I said. 'Safe as the Tower of London – the protectors of all England are there.' 'Ah, there's where the danger is!' she returned. 'If you meet some desperate man, a deserter with his rifle in his hand perhaps, do you think he would hesitate about knocking you over to save himself and at the same time get a little money to help him on his way?'

I smiled at her simulated anxiety for my safety, and set forth when it was very dark but under a fine starry sky. The silence, too, was very profound: there was no good-bye from crowing cock or hooting owl on this occasion, nor did any cyclist pass me on the road with a flash of light from his lamp and a tinkle from his bell. The long straight road on the high down was a dim grey band visible but a few yards before me, lying across the intense blackness of the earth. By day I prefer as a rule walking on the turf, but this road had a rare and peculiar charm at this time. It was now the season when the bird's-foot trefoil, one of the commonest plants of the downland country, was in its fullest bloom, so that in many places the green or grey-green turf as far as one could see on every side was sprinkled and splashed with orange-yellow. Now this creeping, spreading plant, like most plants that grow on the close-cropped sheep-walks, whose safety lies in their power to root themselves and live very close to the surface, yet must ever strive to lift its flowers into the unobstructed light and air and to overtop or get away from its crowding neighbours. On one side of the road, where the turf had been cut by the spade in a sharp line, the plant had found a rare opportunity to get space and light and had thrust out such a multitude of bowering sprays, projecting them beyond the turf, as to form a close band or rope of orange-yellow, which divided the white road from the green turf, and at one spot extended unbroken for upwards of a mile. The effect was so singular and pretty that I had haunted this road for days for the pleasure of seeing that flower border made by nature. Now all colour was extinguished: beneath and around me there was a dimness which at a few yards' distance deepened to blackness, and above me the pale dim blue sky sprinkled with stars; but as I walked I had the image of that brilliant band of yellow colour in my mind.

By-and-by the late moon rose, and a little later the east began to grow lighter and the dark down to change imperceptibly to dim hoary green. Then the exquisite colours of the dawn once more, and the larks rising in the dim distance – a beautiful unearthly sound – and so in the end I came to 'The Stones,' rejoicing, in spite of a cloud which now appeared on the eastern horizon to prevent the coming sun from being seen, that I had the place to myself. The rejoicing came a little too soon; a very few minutes later other visitors on foot and on bicycles began to come in, and we all looked at each other a little blankly. Then a motor-car arrived, and two gentlemen stepped out and stared at us, and one suddenly burst out laughing.

'I see nothing to laugh at!' said his companion a little severely.

The other in a low voice made some apology or explanation which I failed to catch. It was, of course, not right; it was indecent to laugh on such an occasion, for we were not of the ebullient sort who go to 'The Stones' at three o'clock in the morning 'for a lark'; but it was very natural in the circumstances, and mentally I laughed myself at the absurdity of the situation. However, the laugher had been rebuked for his levity, and this incident over, there was nothing further to disturb me or any one in our solemn little gathering.

It was a very sweet experience, and I cannot say that my early morning outing would have been equally good at any other lonely spot on Salisbury Plain or anywhere else with a wide starry sky above me, the flush of dawn in the east, and the larks rising heavenward out of the dim misty earth. Those rudely fashioned immemorial stones standing dark and large against the pale clear moonlit sky imparted something to the feeling. I sat among them alone and had them all to myself, as the others, fearing to tear their clothes on the barbed wire, had not ventured to follow me when I got through the fence. Outside the enclosure they were some distance from me, and as they talked in subdued tones, their voices reached me as a low murmur – a sound not out of harmony with the silent solitary spirit of the place; and there was now no other sound except that of a few larks singing fitfully a long way off.

Just what the element was in that morning's feeling which Stonehenge contributed I cannot say. It was too vague and uncertain, too closely interwoven with the more common feeling for nature. No doubt it was partly due to many untraceable associations, and partly to a thought, scarcely definite enough to be called a thought, of man's life in this land from the time this hoary temple was raised down to the beginning of history. A vast span, a period of ten or more, probably of twenty centuries, during which great things occurred and great tragedies were enacted, which seem all the darker and more tremendous to the mind because unwritten and unknown. But with the mighty dead of these blank ages I could not commune. Doubtless they loved and hated and rose and fell, and there were broken hearts and broken lives; but as beings of flesh and blood we cannot visualize them, and are in doubt even as to their race. And of their minds, or their philosophy of life, we know absolutely nothing. We are able, as Clifford has said in his *Cosmic Emotion*, to shake hands with the ancient Greeks across the great desert of centuries which divides our day from theirs; but there is no shaking hands with these ancients of Britain – or Albion, seeing that we are on the chalk. To our souls they are as strange as the builders of Tiuhuanaco, or Mitla and Itzana, and the cyclopean ruins of Zimbabwe and the Carolines.

It is thought by some of our modern investigators of psychic phenomena that apparitions result from the coming out of impressions left in the surrounding matter, or perhaps in the ether pervading it, especially in moments of supreme agitation or agony. The apparition is but a restored picture, and pictures of this sort are about us in millions; but for our peace they are rarely visible, as the ability to see them is the faculty of but a few persons in certain moods and certain circumstances. Here, then, if anywhere in England, we, or the persons who are endowed with this unpleasant gift, might look for visions of the time when Stonehenge was the spiritual capital, the Mecca of the faithful (when all were that), the meeting-place of all the intellect, the hoary experience, the power and majesty of the land.

But no visions have been recorded. It is true that certain stories of alleged visions have been circulated during the last few years. One, very pretty and touching, is of a child from the London slums who saw things invisible to others. This was one of the children of the very poor, who are taken in summer and planted all about England in cottages to have a week or a fortnight of country air and sunshine. Taken to Stonehenge, she had a vision of a great gathering of people, and so real did they seem that she believed in the reality of it all, and so beautiful did they appear to her that she was reluctant to leave, and begged to be taken back to see it all again. Unfortunately it is not true. A full and careful inquiry has been made into the story, of which there are several versions, and its origin traced to a little story-telling Wiltshire boy who had read or heard of the white-robed priests of the ancient days at 'The Stones,' and who just to astonish other little boys naughtily pretended that he had seen it all himself!

CHAPTER TWENTY-THREE

Following a River

The stream invites us to follow: the impulse is so common that it might be set down as an instinct; and certainly there is no more fascinating pastime than to keep company with a river from its source to the sea. Unfortunately this is not easy in a country where running waters have been enclosed, which should be as free as the rain and sunshine to all, and were once free, when England was England still, before landowners annexed them, even as they annexed or stole the commons and shut up the footpaths and made it an offence for a man to go aside from the road to feel God's grass under his feet. Well, they have also got the road now, and cover and blind and choke us with its dust and insolently hoot-hoot at us. Out of the way, miserable crawlers, if you don't want to be smashed!

Sometimes the way is cut off by huge thorny hedges and fences of barbed wire – man's devilish improvement on the bramble – brought down to the water's edge. The river-follower must force his way through these obstacles, in most cases greatly to the detriment of his clothes and temper; or, should they prove impassable, he must undress and go into the water. Worst of all is the thought that he is a trespasser. The pheasants crow loudly lest he should forget it. Occasionally, too, in these private places he encounters men in velveteens with guns under their arms, and other men in tweeds and knickerbockers, with or without guns, and they all stare at him with amazement in their eyes, like disturbed cattle in a pasture; and sometimes they challenge him. But I must say that, although I have been sharply spoken to on several occasions, always, after a few words, I have been permitted to keep on my way. And on that way I intend to keep until I have no more strength to climb over fences and force my way through hedges, but like a blind and worn-out old badger must take to my earth and die.

I found the Exe easy to follow at first. Further on exceedingly difficult in places; but I was determined to keep near it, to have it behind me and before me and at my side, following, leading, a beautiful silvery serpent that was my friend and companion. For I was following not the Exe only, but a dream as well, and a memory. Before I knew it the Exe was a beloved stream. Many rivers had I seen in my wanderings, but never one to compare with this visionary river, which yet existed, and would be found and followed at last. My forefathers had dwelt for generations beside it, listening all their lives long to its music, and when they left it they still loved it in exile, and died at last with its music in their ears. Nor did the connection end there; their children and children's children doubtless had some inherited memory of it; or how came I to have this feeling, which made it sacred, and drew me to it? We inherit not from our ancestors only, but, through them, something, too, from the earth and place that knew them.

I sought for and found it where it takes its rise on open Exmoor; a simple moorland stream, not wild and foaming and leaping over rocks, but flowing gently between low peaty banks, where the little lambs leap over it from side to side in play. Following the stream down, I come at length to Exford. Here the aspect of the country begins to change; it is not all brown desolate heath; there are green flowery meadows by the river, and some wood. A little further down and the Exe will be a woodland stream; but of all the rest of my long walk I shall only say that to see the real beauty of this stream one must go to Somerset. From Exford to Dulverton it runs, singing aloud, foam-flecked, between high hills clothed to their summits in oak woods: after its union with the Barle it enters Devonshire as a majestic stream, and flows calmly through a rich green country; its wild romantic charm has been left behind.

The uninformed traveller, whose principle it is never to look at a guide-book, is surprised to find that the small village of Exford contains no fewer than half a dozen inns. He asks how they are kept going; and the natives, astonished at his ignorance, proceed to enlighten him. Exford is the headquarters of the stag-hunt: thither the hunters flock in August, and spend so much money during thir brief season that the innkeepers grow rich and fat, and for the rest of the year can afford to doze peacefully behind their bars. Here are the kennels, and when I visited them they contained forty or fifty couples of stag-hounds. These are gigantic foxhounds, selected for their great size from packs all over the country. When out exercising these big vari-coloured dogs make a fine show. It is curious to find that, although these individual variations are continually appearing – very large dogs born of dogs of medium size – others cannot be bred from them; the variety cannot be fixed.

The village is not picturesque. Its one perennial charm is the swift river that flows through it, making music on its wide sandy and pebbly floor. Hither and thither flit the wagtails, finding little half-uncovered stones in the current to perch upon. Both the pied and grey species are there; and, seeing them together, one naturally wishes to resettle for himself the old question as to which is the prettiest and most graceful. Now this one looks best and now that; but the delicately coloured grey and yellow bird has the longest tail and can use it more prettily. Her tail is as much to her, both as ornament and to express emotions, as a fan to any flirtatious Spanish señora. One always thinks of these dainty feathered creatures as females. It would seem quite natural to call the wagtail 'lady-bird,' if that name had not been registered by a diminutive podgy tortoise-shaped black and red beetle.

So shallow is the wide stream in the village that a little girl of about seven came down from a cottage, and to cool her feet waded out into the middle, and there she stood for some minutes on a low flat stone, looking down on her own wavering image broken by a hundred hurrying wavelets and ripples. This small maidie, holding up her short, shabby frock with her wee hands, her bright brown hair falling over her face as she bent her head down and laughed to see her bare little legs and their flickering reflection beneath, made a pretty picture. Like the wagtails, she looked in harmony with her surroundings.

So many are the villages, towns, and places of interest seen, so many the adventures met with in this walk, starting with the baby streamlet beyond Simonsbath, and following it down to Exeter and Exmouth, that it would take half a volume to describe them, however briefly. Yet at the end I found that Exford had left the most vivid and lasting impression, and was remembered with most pleasure. It was more to me than Winsford, that fragrant, cool, grey and green village, the home of immemorial peace, second to no English village in beauty; with its hoary church tower, its great trees, its old stone, thatched cottages draped in ivy and vine, its soothing sound of running waters. Exeter itself did not impress me so strongly, in spite of its cathedral. The village of Exford printed itself thus sharply on my mind because I had there been filled with wonder and delight at the sight of a face exceeding in loveliness all the faces seen in that West Country – a rarest human gem, which had the power of imparting to its setting something of its own wonderful lustre. The type was a common Somerset one, but with marked differences in some respects, else it could not have been so perfect.

W. H. HUDSON

The type I speak of is a very distinct one: in a crowd in a London street you can easily spot a Somerset man who has this mark on his countenance, but it shows more clearly in the woman. There are more types than one, but the variety is less than in other places; the women are more like each other, and differ more from those that are outside their borders than is the case in other English counties. A woman of this prevalent type, to be met with anywhere from Bath and Bedminster to the wilds of Exmoor, is of a good height, and has a pleasant, often a pretty face; regular features, the nose straight, rather long, with thin nostrils; eyes grey-blue; hair brown, neither dark nor light, in many cases with a sandy or sunburnt tint. Black, golden, reds, chestnuts are rarely seen. There is always colour in the skin, but not deep; as a rule it is a light tender brown with a rosy or reddish tinge. Altogether it is a winning face, with smiling eyes; there is more in it of that something we can call 'refinement' than is seen in women of the same class in other counties. The expression is somewhat infantile; a young woman, even a middle-aged woman, will frequently remind you of a little girl of seven or eight summers. The innocent eyes and mobile mouth are singularly childlike. This peculiarity is the more striking when we consider the figure. This is not fully developed according to the accepted standards the hips are too small, the chest too narrow and flat, the arms too thin. True or false, the idea is formed of a woman of a childlike, affectionate nature, but lacking in passion, one to be chosen for a sister rather than a wife. Something in us – instinct or tradition – will have it that the well-developed woman is richest in the purely womanly qualities – the wifely and maternal feelings. The luxuriant types that abound most in Devonshire are not common here.

It will be understood that the women described are those that live in cottages. Here, as elsewhere, as you go higher in the social scale – further from the soil as it were – the type becomes less and less distinct. Those of the 'higher class,' or 'better class,' are few, and always in a sense foreigners.

CHAPTER TWENTY-FOUR

Troston

I doubt if the name of this small Suffolk village, remote from towns and railroads, will have any literary associations for the reader, unless he be a person of exceptionally good memory, who has taken a special interest in the minor poets of the last century; or that it would help him if I add the names of Honington and Sapiston, two other small villages a couple of miles from Troston, with the slow sedgy Little Ouse, or a branch of it, flowing between them. Yet Honington was the birthplace of Robert Bloomfield, known as '*the* Suffolk poet' in the early part of the last century (although Crabbe was living then and was great, as he is becoming again after many years); while at Sapiston, the rustic village on the other side of the old stone bridge, he acquired that love of nature and intimate knowledge of farm life and work which came out later in his *Farmer's Boy*. Finally, Troston, the little village in which I write, was the home of Capel Lofft, a person of importance in his day, who discovered Bloomfield, found a publisher for his poems, and boomed it with amazing success.

I dare say it will only provoke a smile of amusement in readers of literary taste when I confess that Bloomfield's memory is dear to me; that only because of this feeling for the forgotten rustic who wrote rhymes I am now here, strolling about in the shade of the venerable trees in Troston Park - the selfsame trees which the somewhat fantastic Capel knew in his day as 'Homer,' 'Sophocles,' 'Virgil,' 'Milton,' and by other names, calling each old oak, elm, ash, and chestnut after one of the immortals.

I can even imagine that the literary man, if he chanced to be a personal friend, would try to save me from myself by begging me not to put anything of this sort into print. He would warn me that it matters nothing that Bloomfield's verse was exceedingly popular for a time, that twenty-five or thirty editions of his *Farmer's Boy* were issued within three years of its publication in 1800 that it contin-ued to be read for half a century afterwards. There are other better tests. Is it alive to-day? What do judges of literature say of it now? Nothing! They smile and that's all. The absurdity of his popularity was felt in his own day. Byron laughed at it; Crabbe growled and

Charles Lamb said he had looked at the Farmer's Boy and it made him sick. Well, nobody wants to look at it now.

Much more might be said very easily on this side; nevertheless, I think I shall go on with my plea for the small verse-maker who has long fallen out; and though I may be unable to make a case out, the kindly critic may find some circumstance to extenuate my folly – to say, in the end, that this appears to be one of the little foolishnesses which might be forgiven.

I must confess at starting that the regard I have for one of his poems, the *Farmer's Boy*, is not wholly a matter of literary taste or the critical faculty; it is also, to some extent, a matter of association, and as the story of how this comes about is rather curious, I will venture to give it.

In the distant days of my boyhood and early youth my chief delight was in nature, and when I opened a book it was to find something about nature in it, especially some expression of the feeling produced in us by nature, which was, in my case, inseparable from seeing and hearing, and was, to me, the most important thing in life. For who could look on earth, water, sky, on living or growing or inanimate things, without experiencing that mysterious uplifting gladness in him! In due time I discovered that the thing I sought for in printed books was to be found chiefly in poetry, that half a dozen lines charged with poetic feeling about nature often gave me more satisfaction than a whole volume of prose on such subjects. Unfortunately this kind of literature was not obtainable in my early home on the then semi-wild pampas. There were a couple of hundred volumes on the shelves – theology, history, biography, philosophy, science, travels, essays, and some old forgotten fiction; but no verse was there, except Shenstone, in a small, shabby, coverless volume. This I read and re-read until I grew sick of bright Roxana tripping o'er the green, or of gentle Delia when a tear bedews her eye to think yon playful kid must die. To my uncultivated mind – for I had never been at school, and lived in the open air with the birds and beasts – this seemed intolerably artificial; for I was like a hungry person who has nothing but kickshaws put before him, and eats because he is hungry until he loathes a food which in its taste confounds the appetite. Never since those distant days have I looked at a Shenstone or even seen his name in print or heard it spoken, without a slight return of that old sensation of nausea. If Shenstone alone had come to me, the desire for poetry would doubtless have been outlived early in life; but there were many passages, some very long, from the poets in various books on the shelves, and these kept my appetite alive. There was Brown's *Philosophy*, for example; and Brown loved to illustrate his point with endless poetic quotations, the only drawback in my case being that they were almost exclusively drawn from Akenside, who was not 'rural.' But there were other books in which other poets were quoted, and of all these the passages which invariably pleased me most were the descriptions of rural sights and sounds.

One day, during a visit to the city of Buenos Ayres, I discovered in a mean street, in the southern part of the town, a second-hand bookshop, kept by an old snuffy spectacled German in a long shabby black coat. I remember him well because he was a very important person to me. It was the first shop of the kind I had seen – I doubt if there was another in the town; and to be allowed to rummage by the hour among this mass of old books on the dusty shelves and heaped on the brick floor was a novel and delightful experience. The books were mostly in Spanish, French, and German, but there were some in English, and among them I came upon Thomson's *Seasons*. I remember the thrill of joy I experienced when I snatched up the small thin octavo in its smooth calf binding. It was the first book in English I ever bought, and to this day when I see a copy of the *Seasons* on a bookstall, which is often enough, I cannot keep my fingers off it and find it hard to resist the temptation to throw a couple of shillings away and take it home. If shillings had not been wanted for bread and cheese I should have had a roomful of copies by now.

Few books have given me more pleasure, and as I still return to it from time to time I do not suppose I shall ever outgrow the feeling, in spite of its having been borne in on me, when I first conversed with readers of poetry in England, that Thomson is no longer read – that he is unreadable.

After such a find I naturally went back many times to burrow in that delightful rubbish heap, and was at length rewarded by the discovery of yet another poem of rural England – the *Farmer's Boy*. I was prepared to like it, for although I did not know anything about the author's early life, the few passages I had come across in quotations in James Rennie's and other old natural history compilations had given me a strong desire to read the whole poem. I certainly did like it – this quiet description in verse of a green spot in England, my spiritual country which so far as I knew I was never destined to see; and that I continue to like it is, as I have said, the reason of my being in this place.

While thus freely admitting that the peculiar circumstances of the case caused me to value this poem, and, in fact, made it very much more to me than it could be to persons born in England with all its poetical literature to browse on, I am at the same time convinced that this is not the sole reason for my regard.

I take it that the *Farmer's Boy* is poetry, not merely slightly poetized prose in the form of verse, although it is undoubtedly poetry of a very humble order.

Mere descriptions of rural scenes do not demand the higher qualities of the poet – imagination and passion. The lower kind of inspiration is, in fact, often better suited to such themes and shows nature by the common light of day, as it were, instead of revealing it as by a succession of lightning flashes. Even among those who confine themselves to this lower plane, Bloomfield is not great: his small flame is constantly sinking and flickering out. But at intervals it burns up again and redeems the work from being wholly commonplace and trivial. He is, in fact, no better than many another small poet who has been devoured by Time since his day, and whose work no person would now attempt to bring back. It is probable, too, that many of these lesser singers whose fame was brief would in their day have deeply resented being placed on a level with the Suffolk peasant-poet. In spite of all this, and of the impossibility of saving most of the verse which is only passably good from oblivion, I still think the *Farmer's Boy* worth preserving for more reasons than one, but chiefly because it is the only work of its kind.

There is no lack of rural poetry – the *Seasons* to begin with and much Thomsonian poetry besides, treating of nature in a general way; then we have innumerable detached descriptions of actual scenes, such as we find scattered throughout Cowper's *Task*, and numberless other works. Besides all this there are the countless shorter poems, each conveying an impression of some particular scene or aspect of nature; the poet of the open air, like the landscape painter, is ever on the look out for picturesque 'bits' and atmospheric effects as a subject. In Bloomfield we get something altogether different – a simple, consistent, and fairly complete account of the country people's toilsome life in a remote agricultural district in England – a small rustic village set amid green and arable fields, woods and common lands.

We have it from the inside by one who had part in it, born and bred to the humble life he described; and, finally, it is not given as a full day-to-day record – photographed as we may say – with all the minute unessential details and repetitions, but as it appeared when looked back upon from a distance, reliving it in memory, the sights and sounds and events which had impressed the boy's mind standing vividly out. Of this lowly poem it may be truly said that it is 'emotion recollected in tranquillity,' to use the phrase invented by Wordsworth when he attempted a definition of poetry generally and signally failed, as Coleridge demonstrated.

It will be said that the facts of Bloomfield's life – that he was a farmer's boy whose daily tasks were to scare the crows, feed the pigs, and forty things besides, and that later, when learning the shoemaker's trade in a London garret, he put these memories together and made them into a poem – are wholly beside the question when we come to judge the work as literature. A peasant poet may win a great reputation in his own day on account of the circumstances of the case, but in the end his work must be tried by the same standards applied in other and in all cases.

There is no getting away from this, and all that remains is to endeavour to show that the poem, although poor as a whole, is not altogether bad, but contains many lines that glow with beautiful poetic feeling, and many descriptive passages which are admirable. Furthermore, I will venture to say that despite the feebleness of a large part of the work (as poetry) it is yet worth preserving in its entirety on account of its unique character. It may be that I am the only person in England able to appreciate it so fully owing to the way in which it first came to my notice, and the critical reader can, if he thinks proper, discount what I am now saying as mere personal feeling. But the case is this: when, in a distant region of the world, I sought for and eagerly read anything I could find relating to country scenes and life in England – the land of my desire – I was never able to get an *extended* and congruous view of it, with a sense of the continuity in human and animal life in its relation to nature. It was all broken up into pieces or 'bits'; it was in detached scenes, vividly reproduced to the inner eye in many cases, but unrelated and unharmonized, like framed pictures of rural subjects hanging on the walls of a room. Even the *Seasons* failed to supply this want, since Thomson in his great work is of no place and abides nowhere, but ranges on eagle's wings over the entire land, and, for the matter of that, over the whole globe. But I did get it in the *Farmer's Boy*. I visualized the whole scene, the entire harmonious life; I was with him from morn till eve always in that same green country with the same sky, cloudy or serene, above me; in the rustic village, at the small church with a thatched roof where the daws nested in the belfry, and the children played and shouted among the gravestones in the churchyard; in woods and green and ploughed fields and the deep lanes – with him and his fellow-toilers, and the animals, domestic and wild, regarding their life and actions from day to day through all the vicissitudes of the year.

The poem, then, appears to fill a place in our poetic literature, or to fill a gap; at all events from the point of view of those who, born and living in distant parts of the earth, still dream of the Old Home. This perhaps accounts for the fact, which I heard at Honington, that most of the pilgrims to Bloomfield's birthplace are Americans.

Bloomfield followed his great example in dividing his poem into the four seasons, and he begins, Thomson-like, with an invitation to the Muse:

> O come, blest spirit, whatsoe'er thou art,
> Thou kindling warmth that hov'rest round my heart.

But happily he does not attempt to imitate the lofty diction of the *Seasons* or *Windsor Forest*, the noble poem from which, I imagine, Thomson derived his sonorous style. He had a humble mind and knew his limitations, and though he adopted the artificial form of verse which prevailed down to his time he was still able to be simple and natural.

'Spring' does not contain much of the best of his work, but the opening is graceful and is not without a touch of pathos in his apologetic description of himself, as Giles, the farmer's boy.

> Nature's sublimer scenes ne'er charmed my eyes
> Nor Science led me ...
> From meaner objects far my raptures flow ...
> Quick-springing sorrows, transient as the dew,
> Delight from trifles, trifles ever new.
> 'Twas thus with Giles; meek, fatherless, and poor,
> Labour his portion ...
> His life was constant, cheerful servitude ...
> Strange to the world, he wore a bashful look,
> The fields his study, Nature was his book.

The farm is described, the farmer, his kind, hospitable master; the animals, the sturdy team, the cows and the small flock of four-score ewes. Ploughing, sowing, and harrowing are described, and the result left to the powers above:

> Yet oft with anxious heart he looks around,
> And marks the first green blade that breaks the ground;
> In fancy sees his trembling oats uprun,
> His tufted barley yellow with the sun.

While his master dreams of what will be, Giles has enough to do protecting the buried grain from thieving rooks and crows; one of the multifarious tasks being to collect the birds that have been shot, for although –

> Their danger well the wary plunderers know
> And place a watch on some conspicuous bough,
> Yet oft the skulking gunner by surprise
> Will scatter death among them as they rise.

'Tis useless, he tells us, to hang these slain robbers about the fields, since in a little while they are no more regarded than the men of rags and straw with sham rifles in their hands. It was for him to shift the dead from place to place, to arrange them in dying attitudes with outstretched wings. Finally, there was the fox, the stealer of dead crows, to be guarded against; and again at eventide Giles must trudge round to gather up his dead and suspend them from twigs out of reach of hungry night-prowlers. Called up at daybreak each morning, he would take his way through deep lanes overarched with oaks to 'fields remote from home' to redistribute his dead birds, then to fetch the cows, and here we have an example of his close naturalist-like observation in his account of the leading cow, the one who coming and going on all occasions is allowed precedence, who maintains her station, 'won by many a broil,' with just pride. A picture of the cool dairy and its work succeeds, and a lament on the effect of the greed and luxury of the over-populous capital which drains the whole country-side of all produce, which makes the Suffolk dairy-wives run mad for cream, leaving nothing but the 'three-times skimmed sky-blue' to make cheese for local consumption. What a cheese it is, that has the virtue of a post, which turns the stoutest blade, and is at last flung in despair into the hog-trough, where

It rests in perfect spite,
Too big to swallow and too hard to bite!

We then come to the sheep, 'for Giles was shepherd too,' and here
there is more evidence of his observant eye when he describes the
character of the animals, also in what follows about the young
lambs, which forms the best passage in this part. I remember that,
when first reading it, being then little past boyhood myself, how
much I was struck by the vivid beautiful description of a crowd of
young lambs challenging each other to a game, especially at a spot
where they have a mound or hillock for a playground which takes
them with a sort of goatlike joyous madness. For how often in those
days I used to ride out to where the flock of one to two thousand
sheep were scattered on the plain, to sit on my pony and watch the
glad romps of the little lambs with keenest delight! I cannot but
think that Bloomfield's fidelity to nature in such pictures as these
does or should count for something in considering his work. He
concludes:

Adown the slope, then up the hillock climb,
Where every mole-hill is a bed of thyme,
There panting stop; yet scarcely can refrain;
A bird, a leaf, will set them off again;
Or if a gale with strength unusual blow,
Scattering the wild-briar roses into snow,
Their little limbs increasing efforts try,
Like a torn rose the fair assemblage fly.

This image of the wind-scattered petals of the wild rose reminds him
bitterly of the destined end of these joyous young lives – his white-
fleeced little fellow-mortals. He sees the murdering butcher coming in
his cart to demand the firstlings of the flock; he cannot suppress a cry
of grief and indignation – he can only strive to shut out the shocking
image from his soul!

'Summer' opens with some reflections on the farmer's life in a prosy
Crabbe-like manner; and here it may be noted that as a rule Bloomfield
no sooner attempts to rise to a general view than he grows flat; and in
like manner he usually fails when he attempts wide prospects and large
effects. He is at his best only when describing scenes and incidents at

the farm in which he himself is a chief actor, as in this part when, after the sowing of the turnip seed, he is sent out to keep the small birds from the ripening corn:

> There thousands in a flock, for ever gay,
> Loud chirping sparrows welcome on the day,
> And from the mazes of the leafy thorn
> Drop one by one upon the bending corn.

Giles trudging along the borders of the field scares them with his brushing-pole, until, overcome by fatigue and heat, he takes a rest by the brake and lying, half in sun and half in shade, his attention is attracted to the minute insect life that swarms about him:

> The small dust-coloured beetle climbs with pain
> O'er the smooth plantain leaf, a spacious plain!
> Thence higher still by countless steps conveyed,
> He gains the summit of a shivering blade,
> And flirts his filmy wings and looks around,
> Exulting in his distance from the ground.

It is one of his little exquisite pictures. Presently his vision is called to the springing lark:

> Just starting from the corn, he cheerly sings,
> And trusts with conscious pride his downy wings;
> Still louder breathes, and in the face of day
> Mounts up and calls on Giles to mark his way.
> Close to his eye his hat he instant bends
> And forms a friendly telescope that lends
> Just aid enough to dull the glaring light
> And place the wandering bird before his sight,
> That oft beneath a light cloud sweeps along;
> Lost for a while yet pours a varied song;
> The eye still follows and the cloud moves by,
> Again he stretches up the clear blue sky,
> His form, his motions, undistinguished quite,
> Save when he wheels direct from shade to light.

In the end he falls asleep, and waking refreshed picks up his poles and starts again brushing round.

Harvesting scenes succeed, with a picture of Mary, the village beauty, taking her share in the work, and how the labourers in their unwonted liveliness and new-found wit

> Confess the presence of a pretty face.

She is very rustic herself in her appearance:

> Her hat awry, divested of her gown,
> Her creaking stays of leather, stout and brown:
> Invidious barrier! why art thou so high,
> When the slight covering of her neck slips by,
> Then half revealing to the eager sight
> Her full, ripe bosom, exquisitely white?

The leather stays have no doubt gone the way of many other dreadful things, even in the most rustic villages in the land; not so the barbarous practice of docking horses' tails, against which he protests in this place when describing the summer plague of flies and the excessive sufferings of the domestic animals, especially of the poor horses deprived of their only defence against such an enemy. At his own little farm there was yet another plague in the form of an old broken-winged gander, 'the pest and tryant of the yard,' whose unpleasant habit it was to go for the beasts and seize them by the fetlocks. The swine alone did not resent the attacks but welcomed them, receiving the assaults as caresses, and stretching themselves out and lying down and closing their pigs' eyes, they would emit grunts of satisfaction, while the triumphant bird, followed by the whole gabbling flock, would trample on the heads of their prostrate foes.

'Autumn' opens bravely:

> Again the year's decline, 'midst storms and floods,
> The thund'ring chase, the yellow fading woods
> Invite my song.

It contains two of the best things in the poem, the first in the opening part, describing the swine in the acorn season, a delightful picture which must be given in full:

> No more the fields with scattered grain supply
> The restless wandering tenants of the sty;

From oak to oak they run with eager haste,
And wrangling share the first delicious taste
Of fallen acorns; yet but thinly found
Till the strong gale has shook them to the ground.
It comes; and roaring woods obedient wave:
Their home well pleased the joint adventurers leave;
The trudging sow leads forth her numerous young,
Playful, and white, and clean, the briars among,
Till briars and thorns increasing fence them round,
Where last year's mould'ring leaves bestrew the ground,
And o'er their heads, loud lashed by furious squalls,
Bright from their cups the rattling treasure falls;
Hot thirsty food; whence doubly sweet and cool
The welcome margin of some rush-grown pool,
The wild duck's lonely haunt, whose jealous eye
Guards every point; who sits prepared to fly,
On the calm bosom of her little lake,
Too closely screened for ruffian winds to shake;
And as the bold intruders press around,
At once she starts and rises with a bound;
With bristles raised the sudden noise they hear,
And ludicrously wild and winged with fear,
The herd decamp with more than swinish speed,
And snorting dash through sedge and rush and reed;
Through tangled thickets headlong on they go,
Then stop and listen for their fancied foe;
The hindmost still the growing panic spreads,
Repeated fright the first alarm succeeds,
Till Folly's wages, wounds and thorns, they reap;
Yet glorying in their fortunate escape,
Their groundless terrors by degrees soon cease,
And Night's dark reign restores their peace.
For now the gale subsides, and from each bough
The roosting pheasant's short but frequent crow
Invites to rest, and huddling side by side
The herd in closest ambush seek to hide;
Seek some warm slope with shagged moss o'erspread,
Dried leaves their copious covering and their bed.

In vain may Giles, through gathering glooms that fall,
And solemn silence, urge his piercing call;
Whole days and nights they tarry 'midst their store,
Nor quit the woods till oaks can yield no more.

It is a delightful passage to one that knows a pig – the animal we respect
for its intelligence, holding it in this respect higher, more human, than
the horse, and at the same time laugh at on account of certain ludicrous
points about it, as for example its liability to lose its head. Thousands
of years of comfortable domestic life have failed to rid it of this incon-
venient heritage from the time when wild in woods it ran. Yet in this
particular instance the terror of the swine does not seem wholly inex-
cusable, if we know a wild duck as well as a pig, especially the duck that
takes to haunting a solitary woodland pool, who, when intruded on,
springs up with such a sudden tremendous splash and flutter of wings
and outrageous screams, that man himself, if not prepared for it, may
be thrown off his balance.

Passing over other scenes, about one hundred and fifty lines, we
come to the second notable passage, when after the sowing of the
winter wheat, poor Giles once more takes up his old occupation of
rook-scaring. It is not now as in spring and summer:

Keen blows the blast, or ceaseless rain descends;
The half-stripped hedge a sorry shelter lends,

and he thinks it would be nice to have a hovel, no matter how small, to
take refuge in, and at once sets about its construction.

In some sequestered nook, embanked around,
Sods for its walls and straw in burdens bound;
Dried fuel hoarded is his richest store,
And circling smoke obscures his little door;
Whence creeping forth to duty's call he yields,
And strolls the Crusoe of the lonely fields.
On whitehorn tow'ring, and the leafless rose,
A frost-nipped feast in bright vermilion glows;
Where clust'ring sloes in glossy order rise,
He crops the loaded branch, a cumbrous prize;
And on the flame the splutt'ring fruit he rests,
Placing green sods to seat his coming guests;

His guests by promise; playmates young and gay:-
But ah! fresh pastures lure their steps away!
He sweeps his hearth, and homeward looks in vain,
Till feeling Disappointment's cruel pain
His fairy revels are exchanged for rage,
His banquet marred, grown dull his hermitage,
The field becomes his prison, till on high
Benighted birds to shades and coverts fly.

'The field becomes his prison,' and the thought of this trivial restraint, which is yet felt so poignantly, brings to mind an infinitely greater one. Look, he says –

From the poor bird-boy with his roasted sloes

to the miserable state of those who are confined in dungeons, deprived of daylight and the sight of the green earth, whose minds perpetually travel back to happy scenes,

Trace and retrace the beaten worn-out way,

whose chief bitterness it is to be forgotten and see no familiar friendly face.

'Winter' is, I think, the best of the four parts it gives the idea that the poem was written as it stands, from 'Spring' onwards, that by the time he got to the last part the writer had acquired a greater ease and assurance. At all events it is less patchy and more equal. It is also more sober in tone, as befits the subject, and opens with an account of the domestic animals on the farm, their increased dependence on man and the compassionate feelings they evoke in us. He is, we feel, dealing with realities, always from the point of view of a boy of sensitive mind and tender heart – one taken in boyhood from this life before it had wrought any change in him. For in due time the farm boy, however fine his spirit may be, must harden and grow patient and stolid in heat and cold and wet, like the horse that draws the plough or cart; and as he hardens he grows callous. In his wretched London garret if any change came to him it was only to an increased love and pity for the beasts he had lived among, who looked and cried to him to be fed. He describes it well, the frost and bitter cold, the hungry cattle following the cart to the fields, the load of turnips thrown out on the hard frozen ground;

but the turnips too are frozen hard and they cannot eat them until Giles, following with his beetle, splits them up with vigorous blows, and the cows gather close round him, sending out a cloud of steam from their nostrils.

The dim short winter day soon ends, but the sound of the flails continues in the barns till long after dark before the weary labourers end their task and trudge home. Giles, too, is busy at this time taking hay to the housed cattle, many a sweet mouthful being snatched from the load as he staggers beneath it on his way to the racks. Then follow the well-earned hours of 'warmth and rest' by the fire in the big old kitchen which he describes:

> For the rude architect, unknown to fame
> (Nor symmetry nor elegance his aim),
> Who spread his floors of solid oak on high,
> On beams rough-hewn from age to age that lie,
> Bade his wide fabric unimpaired sustain
> The orchard's store, and cheese, and golden grain;
> Bade from its central base, capacious laid,
> The well-wrought chimney rear its lofty head
> Where since hath many a savoury ham been stored,
> And tempests howled and Christmas gambols roared.

The tired ploughman, steeped in luxurious heat, by and by falls asleep and dreams sweetly until his chilblains or the snapping fire awakes him, and he pulls himself up and goes forth yawning to give his team their last feed, his lantern throwing a feeble gleam on the snow as he makes his way to the stable. Having completed his task, he pats the sides of those he loves best by way of good-night, and leaves them to their fragrant meal. And this kindly action on his part suggests one of the best passages of the poem. Even old well-fed Dobbin occasionally rebels against his slavery, and released from his chains will lift his clumsy hoofs and kick, 'disdainful of the dirty wheel.' Short-sighted Dobbin!

> Thy chains were freedom, and thy toils repose,
> Could the poor post-horse tell thee all his woes;
> Show thee his bleeding shoulders, and unfold
> The dreadful anguish he endures for gold;
> Hired at each call of business, lust, or rage,

That prompts the traveller on from stage to stage.
Still on *his* strength depends their boasted speed;
For them his limbs grow weak, his bare ribs bleed;
And though he groaning quickens at command,
Their extra shilling in the rider's hand
Becomes his bitter scourge ...

The description, too long to quote, which follows of the tortures inflicted on the post-horse a century ago, is almost incredible to us, and we flatter ourselves that such things would not be tolerated now. But we must get over the ground somehow, and I take it that but for the invention of other more rapid means of transit the present generation would be as little concerned at the pains of the post-horse as they are at the horrors enacted behind the closed doors of the physiological laboratories, the atrocity of the steel trap, the continual murdering by our big game hunters of all the noblest animals left on the globe, and finally the annual massacre of millions of beautiful birds in their breeding time to provide ornaments for the hats of our women.

'Come forth he must,' says Bloomfield, when he describes how the flogged horse at length gains the end of the stage and, 'trembling under complicated pains,' when 'every nerve a separate anguish knows,' he is finally unharnessed and led to the stable door, but has scarcely tasted food and rest before he is called for again.

Though limping, maimed and sore;
He hears the whip; the chaise is at the door ...
The collar tightens and again he feels
His half-healed wounds inflamed; again the wheels
With tiresome sameness in his ears resound
O'er blinding dust or miles of flinty ground.

This is over and done with simply because the post-horse is no longer wanted, and we have to remember that no form of cruelty inflicted, whether for sport or profit or from some other motive, on the lower animals has ever died out of itself in the land. Its end has invariably been brought about by legislation through the devotion of men who were the 'cranks,' the 'faddists,' the 'sentimentalists,' of their day, who were jeered and laughed at by their fellows, and who only succeeded by sheer tenacity and force of character after long fighting against public opinion and a reluctant Parliament, in finally getting their law.

Bloomfield's was but a small voice crying in the wilderness, and he was indeed a small singer in the day of our greatest singers. As a poet he was not worthy to unloose the buckles of their shoes; but he had one thing in common with the best and greatest, the feeling of tender love and compassion for the lower animals which was in Thomson and Cowper, but found its highest expression in his own great contemporaries, Coleridge, Shelley, and Wordsworth. In virtue of this feeling he was of their illustrious brotherhood.

In conclusion, I will quote one more passage. From the subject of horses he passes to that of dogs and their occasional reversion to wildness, when the mastiff or cur, the 'faithful' house-dog by day, takes to sheep-killing by night. As a rule he is exceedingly cunning, committing his depredations at a distance frown home, and after getting his fill of slaughter he sneaks home in the early hours to spend the day in his kennel 'licking his guilty paws.' This is an anxious time for shepherds and farmers, and poor Giles is compelled to pay late evening visits to his small flock of heavy-sided ewes penned in their distant fold. It is a comfort to him to have a full moon on these lonely expeditions, and despite his tremors he is able to appreciate the beauty of the scene.

> With saunt'ring steps he climbs the distant stile,
> Whilst all around him wears a placid smile;
> There views the white-robed clouds in clusters driven
> And all the glorious pageantry of heaven.
> Low on the utmost bound'ry of the sight
> The rising vapours catch the silver light;
> Thence Fancy measures, as they parting fly
> Which first will throw its shadow on the eye,
> Passing the source of light; and thence away,
> Succeeded quick by brighter still than they.
> For yet above the wafted clouds are seen
> (In a remoter sky still more serene)
> Others detached in ranges through the air,
> Spotless as snow and countless as they're fair;
> Scattered immensely wide from east to west
> The beauteous semblance of a flock at rest.

This is almost the only passage in the poem in which something of the vastness of visible nature is conveyed. He saw the vastness only in the sky on nights with a full moon or when he made a telescope of his hat to watch the flight of the lark. It was not a hilly country about his native place, and his horizon was a very limited one, usually bounded by the hedgerow timber at the end of the level field. The things he depicts were seen at short range, and the poetry, we see, was of a very modest kind. It was a 'humble note' which pleased me in the days of long ago when I was young and very ignorant, and as it pleases me still it may be supposed that mentally I have not progressed with the years. Nevertheless, I am not incapable of appreciating the greater music; all that is said in its praise, even to the extremest expressions of admiration of those who are moved to a sense of wonder by it, find an echo in me. But it is not only a delight to me to listen to the lark singing at heaven's gate and to the vesper nightingale in the oak copse – the singer of a golden throat and wondrous artistry; I also love the smaller vocalists – the modest shufewing and the lesser whitethroat and the yellowhammer with his simple chant. These are very dear to me: their strains do not strike me as trivial; they have a lesser distinction of their own and I would not miss them from the choir. The literary man will smile at this and say that my paper is naught but an idle exercise, but I fancy I shall sleep the better tonight for having discharged this ancient debt which has been long on my conscience.

CHAPTER TWENTY-FIVE

My Friend Jack

My friend Jack is a retriever – very black, very curly, perfect in shape, but just a retriever; and he is really not my friend, only he thinks he is, which comes to the same thing. So convinced is he that I am his guide, protector, and true master, that if I were to give him a downright scolding or even a thrashing he would think it was all right and go on just the same. His way of going on is to make a companion of me whether I want him or not. I do not want him, but his idea is that I want him very much. I bitterly blame myself for having made the first advances, although nothing came of it except that he growled. I met him in a Cornish village in a house where I stayed. There was a nice kennel there, painted green, with a bed of clean straw and an empty plate which had contained his dinner, but on peeping in I saw no dog. Next day it was the same, and the next, and the day after that; then I inquired about it – Was there a dog in that house or not? Oh, yes, certainly there was: Jack, but a very independent sort of dog. On most days he looked in, ate his dinner and had a nap on his straw, but he was not what you would call a home-keeping dog.

One day I found him in, and after we had looked for about a minute at each other, I squatting before the kennel, he with chin on paws pretending to be looking through me at something beyond, I addressed a few kind words to him, which he received with the before-mentioned growl. I pronounced him a surly brute and went away. It was growl for growl. Nevertheless I was well pleased at having escaped the consequences in speaking kindly to him. I am not a 'doggy' person nor even a canophilist. The purely parasitic or degenerate pet dog moves me to compassion, but the natural vigorous outdoor dog I fear and avoid because we are not in harmony; consequently I suffer and am a loser when he forces his company on me. The outdoor world I live in is not the one to which a man goes for a constitutional, with a dog to save him from feeling lonely, or, if he has a gun, with a dog to help him kill something. It is a world which has sound in it, distant cries and penetrative calls, and low mysterious notes, as of insects and corncrakes, and frogs chirping and of grasshopper warblers – sounds like wind in the dry sedges. And there are also sweet and beautiful songs; but it is very quiet world where creatures move about subtly, on wings, on polished scales, on softly padded feet – rabbits, foxes, stoats, weasels, and voles and birds and lizards and adders and slow-worms, also beetles and dragon-flies. Many are at enmity with each other, but on account of their quietude there is no disturbance, no outcry and rushing into hiding. And having acquired this habit from them I am able to see and be with them. The sitting bird, the frolicking rabbit, the basking adder – they are as little disturbed at my presence as the butterfly that drops down close to my feet to sun his wings on a leaf or frond and makes me hold my breath at the sight of his divine colour, as if he had just fluttered down from some brighter realm in the sky. Think of a dog in this world, intoxicated with the odours of so many wild creatures, dashing and splashing through bogs and bushes! It is ten times worse than a bull in a china-shop. The bull can but smash a lot of objects made of baked clay; the dog introduces a mad panic in a world of living intelligent beings, a fairy realm of exquisite beauty. They scuttle away and vanish into hiding as if a deadly wind had blown over the earth and swept them out of existence. Only the birds remain – they can fly and do not fear for their own lives, but are in a state of intense anxiety about their eggs and young among the bushes which he is dashing through or exploring.

I had good reason, then, to congratulate myself on Jack's surly behaviour on our first meeting. Then, a few days later, a curious thing happened. Jack was discovered one morning in his kennel, and when spoken to came or rather dragged himself out, a most pitiable object. He was horribly bruised and sore all over; his bones appeared to be all broken; he was limp and could hardly get on his feet, and in that miserable condition he continued for some three days.

At first we thought he had been in a big fight – he was inclined that way, his master said – but we could discover no tooth marks or lacerations, nothing but bruises. Perhaps, we said, he had fallen into the hands of some cruel person in one of the distant moorland farms, who had tied him up, then thrashed him with a big stick, and finally turned him loose to die on the moor or crawl home if he could. His master looked so black at this that we said no more about it. But Jack was a wonderfully tough dog, all gristle I think, and after three days of lying there like a dead dog he quickly recovered, though I'm quite sure that if his injuries had been distributed among any half-dozen pampered or pet dogs it would have killed them all. A morning came when the kennel was empty: Jack was not dead – he was well again, and, as usual, out.

Just then I was absent for a week or ten days then, back again, I went out one fine morning for a long day's ramble along the coast. A mile or so from home, happening to glance back I caught sight of a black dog's face among the bushes thirty or forty yards away gazing earnestly at me. It was Jack, of course, nothing but his head visible in an opening among the bushes – a black head which looked as if carved in ebony, in a wonderful setting of shining yellow furze blossoms. The beauty and singularity of the sight made it impossible for me to be angry with him, though there's nothing a man more resents than being shadowed, or secretly followed and spied upon, even by a dog, so, without considering what I was letting myself in for, I cried out 'Jack' and instantly he bounded out and came to my side, then flew on ahead, well pleased to lead the way.

'I must suffer him this time,' I said resignedly, and went on, he always ahead acting as my scout and hunter – self-appointed, of course, but as I had not ordered him back in trumpet tones and hurled a rock at him to enforce the command, he took it that he was appointed by me. He certainly made the most of his position; no one could say that he was lacking in zeal. He scoured the country to the right and left and far in advance of me, crashing through furze thickets and splashing across bogs and streams, spreading terror where he went and leaving nothing for me to look at. So it went on until after one o'clock when, tired and hungry, I was glad to go down into a small fishing cove to get some dinner in a cottage I knew. Jack threw himself down on the floor and shared my meal, then made friends with the fisherman's wife and got a second meal of saffron cake which, being a Cornish dog, he thoroughly enjoyed.

The second half of the day was very much like the first, altogether a blank day for me, although a very full one for Jack, who had filled a vast number of wild creatures with terror, furiously hunted a hundred or more, and succeeded in killing two or three.

Jack was impossible, and would never be allowed to follow me again. So I sternly said and so thought, but when the time came and I found him waiting for me his brown eyes bright with joyful anticipation, I could not scowl at him and thunder out No! I could not help putting myself in his place. For here he was, a dog of boundless energy who must exercise his powers or be miserable, with nothing in the village for him except to witness the not very exciting activities of others; and that, I discovered, had been his life. He was mad to do something, and because there was nothing for him to do his time was mostly spent in going about the village to keep an eye on the movements of the people, especially of those who did the work, always with the hope that his services might be required in some way by someone. He was grateful for the smallest crumbs, so to speak. House-work and work about the house – milking, feeding the pigs and so on – did not interest him, nor would he attend the labourers in the fields. Harvest time would make a difference; now it was ploughing, sowing, and hoeing, with nothing for Jack. But he was always down at the fishing cove to see the boats go out or come in and join in the excitement when there was a good catch. It was still better when the boat went with provisions to the lighthouse, or to relieve the keeper, for then Jack would go too and if they would not have him he would plunge into the waves and swim after it until the sails were hoisted and it flew like a great gull from him and he was compelled to swim back to land. If there was nothing else to do he would go to the stone quarry and keep the quarrymen company, sharing their dinner and hunting away the cows and donkeys that came too near. Then at six o'clock he would turn up at the cricket-field, where a few young enthusiasts would always attend to practise after working hours.

Living this way Jack was, of course, known to everybody – as well known as the burly parson, the tall policeman, and the lazy girl who acted as postman and strolled about the parish once a day delivering the letters. When Jack trotted down the village street he received as many greetings as any human inhabitant – 'Hullo, Jack!' or 'Morning, Jack,' or 'Where be going, Jack?'

But all this variety, and all he could do to fit himself into and be a part of the village life and fill up his time, did not satisfy him. Happiness for Jack was out on the moor – its lonely wet thorny places, pregnant with fascinating scents, not of flowers and odorous herbs, but of alert, warm-blooded, and swift-footed creatures. And I was going there – would I, could I, be so heartless as to refuse to take him?

You see that Jack, being a dog, could not go there alone. He was a social being by instinct as well as training, dependent on others, or on the one who was his head and master. His human master, or the man who took him out and spoke to him in a tone of authority, represented the head of the pack – the leading dog for the time being, albeit a dog that walked on his hind legs and spoke a bow-wow dialect of his own.

I thought of all this and of many things besides. The dog, I remembered, was taken by man out of his own world and thrust into one where he can never adapt himself perfectly to the conditions, and it was consequently nothing more than simple justice on my part to do what I could to satisfy his desire even at some cost to myself. But while I was revolving the matter in my mind, feeling rather unhappy about it, Jack was quite happy, since he had nothing to revolve. For him it was all settled and done with. Having taken him out once, I must go on taking him out always. Our two lives, hitherto running apart – his in the village, where he occupied himself with uncongenial affairs, mine on the moor where, having but two legs to run on, I could catch no rabbits – were now united in one current to our mutual advantage. His habits were altered to suit the new life. He stayed in now so as not to lose me when I went for a walk, and when returning, instead of going back to his kennel, he followed me in and threw himself down, all wet, on the rug before the fire. His master and mistress came in and stared in astonishment. It was against the rules of the house! They ordered him out and he looked at them without moving. Then they spoke again very sharply indeed, and he growled a low buzzing growl without lifting his chin from his paws, and they had to leave him! He had transferred his allegiance to a new master and head of the pack. He was under my protection and felt quite safe: if I had taken any part in that scene it would have been to order those two persons who had once lorded it over him out of the room!

I didn't really mind his throwing over his master and taking possession of the rug in my sitting-room, but I certainly did very keenly resent his behaviour towards the birds every morning at breakfast-time. It was my chief pleasure to feed them during the bad weather, and it was often a difficult task even before Jack came on the scene to mix himself in my affairs. The Land's End is, I believe, the windiest place in the world, and when I opened the window and threw the scraps out the wind would catch and whirl them away like so many feathers over the garden wall, and I could not see what became of them. It was necessary to go out by the kitchen door at the back (the front door facing the sea being impossible) and scatter the food on the lawn, and then go into watch the result from behind the window. The blackbirds and thrushes would wait for a lull to fly in over the wall, while the daws would hover overhead and sometimes succeed in dropping down and seizing a crust, but often enough when descending they would be caught and whirled away by the blast. The poor magpies found their long tails very much against them in the scramble, and it was even worse with the pied wagtail. He would go straight for the bread and get whirled and tossed about the smooth lawn like a toy bird made of feathers, his tail blown over his head. It was bad enough, and then Jack, curious about these visits to the lawn, came to investigate and finding the scraps, proceeded to eat them all up. I tried to make him understand better by feeding him before I fed the birds; then by scolding and even hitting him, but he would not see it; he knew better than I did; he wasn't hungry and he didn't want bread, but he would eat it all the same, every scrap of it, just to prevent it from being wasted. Jack was doubtless both vexed and amused at my simplicity in thinking that all this food which I put on the lawn would remain there undevoured by those useless creatures the birds until it was wanted.

Even this I forgave him, for I saw that he had not, that with his dog mind he could not, understand me. I also remembered the words of a wise old Cornish writer with regard to the mind of the lower animals: 'But their faculties of mind are no less proportioned to their state of subjection than the shape and properties of their bodies. They have knowledge peculiar to their several spheres and sufficient for the underpart they have to act.'

Let me be free from the delusion that it is possible to raise them above this level, or in other words to add an inch to their mental stature. I have nothing to forgive Jack after all. And so in spite of everything Jack was suffered at home and accompanied me again and again in my walks abroad; and there were more blank days, or if not altogether blank, seeing that there was Jack himself to be observed and thought about, they were not the kind of days I had counted on having. My only consolation was that Jack failed to capture more than one out of every hundred, or perhaps five hundred, of the creatures he hunted, and that I was even able to save a few of these. But I could not help admiring his tremendous energy and courage, especially in cliff-climbing when we visited the headlands – those stupendous masses and lofty piles of granite which rise like castles built by giants of old. He would almost make me tremble for his life when, after climbing on to some projecting rock, he would go to the extreme end and look down over it as if it pleased him to watch the big waves break in foam on the black rocks a couple of hundred feet below. But it was not the big green waves or any sight in nature that drew him – he sniffed and sniffed and wriggled and twisted his black nose, and raised and depressed his ears as he sniffed, and was excited solely because the upward currents of air brought him tidings of living creatures that lurked in the rocks below – badger and fox and rabbit. One day when quitting one of these places, on looking up I spied Jack standing on the summit of a precipice about seventy-five feet high. Jack saw me and waved his tail, and then started to come straight down to me! From the top a faint rabbit track was, visible winding downwards to within twenty-four feet of the ground; the rest was a sheer wall of rock. Down he dashed, faster and faster as he got to where the track ended, and then losing his footing he fell swiftly to the earth, but luckily dropped on a deep spongy turf and was not hurt. After witnessing this reckless act I knew how he had come by those frightful bruises on a former occasion. He had doubtless fallen a long way down a cliff and had been almost crushed on the stones. But the lesson was lost on Jack; he would have it that where rabbits and foxes went he could go!

After all, the chief pleasure those blank bad days had for me was the thought that Jack was as happy as he could well be. But it was not enough to satisfy me, and by and by it came into my mind that I had been long enough at that place. It was hard to leave Jack, who had put himself so entirely in my hands, and trusted me so implicitly. But – the weather was keeping very bad: was there ever known such a June as this of 1907? So wet and windy and cold! Then, too, the bloom had gone from the furze. It was, I remembered, to witness this chief loveliness that I came. Looking on the wide moor and far-off boulder-strewn hills and seeing how rusty the bushes were, I quoted:

The bloom has gone, and with the bloom go I,

and early in the morning, with all my belongings on my back, I stole softly forth, glancing apprehensively in the direction of the kennel, and out on to the windy road. It was painful to me to have to decamp in this way; it made me think meanly of myself; but if Jack could read this and could speak his mind I think he would acknowledge that my way of bringing the connection to an end was best for both of us. I was not the person, or dog on two legs, he had taken me for, one with a proper desire to kill things: I only acted according to my poor lights. Nothing, then, remains to be said except that one word which it was not convenient to speak on the windy morning of my departure – Good-bye, Jack.